DYLAN
THOMAS

# Under Milk Wood

Images by
PETER
BLAKE

# THE HEART'S GRANARY

Michael Craig-Martin, *Book*, letterpress print from the *de luxe* edition
of *Drawing* (2015)

# THE HEART'S GRANARY

Poetry and Prose from
Fifty Years of Enitharmon Press

*Compiled by Lawrence Sail*

ENITHARMON PRESS

*Enitharmon Friends Patrons*
Colin Beer, Duncan Forbes, Sean O'Connor, Masa Ohtake

———

First published in 2017
by Enitharmon Press
10 Bury Place
London WC1A 2JL

www.enitharmon.co.uk

Distributed in the UK by
Central Books
50 Freshwater Road
Chadwell Heath, RM8 1RX

Distributed in the USA and Canada
by Independent Publishers Group
814 North Franklin Street
Chicago, IL 60610
USA
www.ipgbooks.com

ISBN: 978-1-911253-28-0 (hardback)
ISBN: 978-1-911253-36-5 (signed limited edition of 50 copies)

British Library Cataloguing-in-Publication Data.
A catalogue record for this book is available
from the British Library.

Designed in Albertina by Libanus Press
and printed in Wales by
Gomer Press

# Introduction

This anthology marks the 50th anniversary of Enitharmon Press. Not a long period of time, in historical terms – but to have sustained and developed an independent publishing house over the course of half a century, in radically shifting technological, social and political contexts, is a formidable achievement, owing much to the fact that Enitharmon has had only two Directors: Alan Clodd for the first twenty years, succeeded by Stephen Stuart-Smith for the next thirty.

Given that every publisher has a particular style and vision, what are the distinctive features of Enitharmon? Perhaps most striking are the range and variety of its publications. In the early years a number of exotic blooms sprang from the new ground, indicative perhaps of a venture establishing its identity by reaching out in various directions. Prominent among these was the appearance, alongside volumes of poems, of a whole series of books by and about George Gissing (a close friend of Alan Clodd's grandfather). There is also Brenda Chamberlain's account of her partnership with John Petts and Alun Lewis (*Alun Lewis & the Making of the Caseg Broadsheets*, 1970); a Lorca prose fragment translated by Kathleen Raine and R. M. Nadal, with two unpublished Lorca drawings (*Sun & Shadow*, 1972); a short story by Borges (*The Congress*, 1974) and, in the same year, two Ronald Firbank stories in French (*La Princesse aux Soleils* and *Harmonie*) with English versions by Edgell Rickword; the beginnings of a series about John Cowper Powys and his brother Llewelyn, with studies by Jeremy Hooker, Kenneth Hopkins and Roland Mathias; and Frederick Rolfe's/Baron Corvo's *Letters to Harry Bainbridge* (1976).

In a longer perspective, Enitharmon has consistently championed and maintained the reputations of a number of writers, notably Frances Bellerby, David Gascoyne, Jeremy Hooker, Jeremy Reed, Edward Upward and Denton Welch. It could be said that it is David Gascoyne who comes close to dominating the list, from the aphorisms published in 1970 as *The Sun at Midnight* via the re-issuing of *A Short Survey of Surrealism* (2000, first published in 1935) to the *Selected Prose 1934–1996* (1998) and the *New Collected Poems* (2014), both edited by Roger Scott. There have been ten other books along the way, including Gascoyne's journals from 1936 to 1939 and his verse translations. Almost as prominent is Kathleen Raine, who encouraged Alan Clodd to set up a publishing business in the first place. One of Enitharmon's two publications in its first year was the text of a speech she gave at the Poetry Society (the other publication was a collection of poems by her daughter, Anna Madge Hopewell), and Raine continued to be a potent presence, her *imprimatur* expressed as an approving foreword or comment for many books. Her influence chimes with the Blakean tendency towards the numinous and visionary already evident in the name chosen for the Press, but it would be wrong to see Enitharmon as limited to this approach. The early list already shows considerable variety, and includes the work of Joseph Chiari, Leonard Clark, Frances Horovitz, Hugo Manning, and John Heath-Stubbs, whose *Artorius* came out in 1973: a striking long poem notable for the verve and energy characteristic of its author. More recently, there have been authoritative *Collected Poems*, among them those of Alan Brownjohn, U. A. Fanthorpe, Phoebe Hesketh, Jeremy Hooker, Frances Horovitz (in conjunction with Bloodaxe Books), Ruth Pitter and Anthony Thwaite. Simon Armitage, Sebastian Barker, Kevin Crossley-Holland, Martyn Crucefix, Neil Curry, Hilary Davies, Jane Duran, Duncan Forbes, Michael Longley, Paul Muldoon, Jeremy Reed and Myra Schneider are all well represented, while the cause of bringing renewed attention to the work of neglected or half-forgotten writers is finely exemplified by the *Selected Poems* of Jack Clemo (2015), Frances Cornford (1996) and George MacBeth (2002), as well as the novels and stories of Denton Welch and Edward Upward. Likewise, the Press has played its part in maintaining the visibility of David Jones, as both artist and writer, in advance of the recent revival of interest in his work.

Enitharmon is notable for its high standards of design and production, most fully realised in the beautiful books appearing under the imprint of Enitharmon Editions. In tandem with the Press, but fiscally separate from it, this associated company produces limited editions, usually letterpress. They include collaborations between well-known artists and writers, and these have benefited greatly from the support and expertise of the art historian Marco Livingstone. Illustrations have been a feature from early on, including drawings, photogravures, etchings, lithographs, photographs and paintings. Christopher Le Brun drawings go alongside Ted Hughes's versions of Ovid; Hughie O'Donoghue's paintings accompany Seamus Heaney's re-telling of *The Testament of Cresseid;* images by Tony Bevan enrich Harold Pinter's *The Disappeared and Other Poems;* those of Jim Dine, the poems of Robert Creeley (*Pictures*); Thom Gunn's poems (*In the Twilight Slot*) have a photographic portrait of the poet by Arthur Tress. And the work of Paula Rego is seen in striking collaborations, including with Blake Morrison (*Pendle Witches*), and in her illustrations for *Jane Eyre* (like a number of Enitharmon Editions books, this is available in a regular edition, too). Many also deserve special mention for the elegance and boldness of their design and covers (see the list of illustrations on pages 20–21), as do the marbled-wrappered chapbooks of work by Dannie Abse, Ronald Blythe, Michael Longley, Paul Muldoon, Edmund White and, most recently, John Montague.

Enitharmon has always published prose as well as poems, and here too the range is impressive – there are essays, studies, memoirs, letters, short stories and novels, even a screenplay (John Banville, *The Sea*). Prose is, by definition, harder to represent fully in an anthology such as this one, but nonetheless constitutes an important component of the press's work. As does translation, from David Gascoyne's and Jeremy Reed's versions of Novalis (*Hymns to the Night*, 1989) to Martyn Crucefix's translations of Rilke (*Duino Elegies,* 2006, and *Sonnets to Orpheus,* 2010) and David Harsent's versions of Yannis Ritsos (*In Secret,* 2012). Equally noteworthy are Jane Duran's and Gloria García Lorca's translations of Lorca's *Gipsy Ballads* (2011), Michael Longley's of various poets (in *Wavelengths,* 2009, with three fine wood engravings by Jeffrey Morgan) and Robin Robertson's versions of Tomas Tranströmer (*The Deleted World,* 2006) – one of four Nobel Prizewinners to have had work published by Enitharmon (the others are Beckett, Heaney and Pinter).

The making of this book has been an emphatic reminder of the remarkable role played in the literary life of the country by independent publishers – most conspicuously Peter Jay at Anvil Press, Neil Astley at Bloodaxe Books and Michael Schmidt at Carcanet. Their work over many years bears witness to astonishing perseverance and dedication. Stephen Stuart-Smith's thirty years as Director of Enitharmon have been similarly heroic.

With the publications of half a century to choose from, including many images and illustrations, selection has been a considerable undertaking. Limitations of space and cost have of course played their part: and a number of longer poems, like a considerable tally of the prose publications, do not easily lend themselves to representation by an extract (the long poems of Hugo Manning are a prime instance). Otherwise, I have straightforwardly chosen what most appeals to me and seems to succeed best on its own ground. At the same time, I have also been keen to convey the range of Enitharmon's publications during the fifty years of its existence. These twin aims have been my principal guides. And while all the selections have been made on the basis of individual merit, an anthology also creates new contexts. It has been intriguing to see how one inclusion might relate to another, and so what might be their ordering – which is thematic, rather than chronological or alphabetical.

There are considerations enough to have kept my feet firmly grounded. As Paul Muldoon asserts in *The Bloodaxe Book of Poetry Quotations* (edited by Dennis O'Driscoll, 2006), 'Anyone who makes an anthology is almost certifiably mad'. If this seems too daunting, in the same book there is also Stephen Romer's apt likening of the anthologist to 'some lumbering beast of burden, whose load is unceasingly increased; there is the slippage and settling of transit, and then some precious stuff falls off, and then whole saddlebags go missing as the century advances'.

The century has not only advanced, but turned: and viewing the last fifty years in the perspective of an anniversary anthology vividly shows up changes in book production and marketing, as well as those in poetic diction and social attitudes. To look through some of the early papers in the Enitharmon archive is to be reminded of the sheer daily slog attending the venture from its outset – not just the processes of selection and production, from the reading of submissions to communications with writers, but keeping records and accounts, dealing with sales representatives, retailers and individual buyers. It is hard to see how Alan Clodd was able to achieve all this in addition to his already full existence as a bookseller, collector and dealer, or indeed how Stephen Stuart-Smith has managed to develop Enitharmon's list as broadly as he has. A clue to their success may lie in the choice of Enitharmon for the name of the press, with its inherent commitment to a central and sustaining vision of poetry – the richness exemplified, even or especially in the face of darkness, by Isaac Rosenberg's cherishing, in 'August, 1914' (see page 104), of 'the heart's dear granary'.

Since 1967 – its spring of large anti-Vietnam War demonstrations in New York and San Francisco; its summer dubbed 'The Summer of Love', with Pablo Neruda receiving the first Viareggio-Versile Prize and the Beatles releasing *Sgt. Pepper's Lonely Hearts Club Band*; its autumn of the Nobel Prize for Literature being awarded to the Argentinian poet Miguel Ángel Asturias, the capture and execution of Che Guevara, and Allen Ginsberg chanting at the Pentagon – since then, the world of writing has undergone changes as fundamental as those in any other sphere. The established bookselling framework of private dealers and independent retail outlets has all but vanished, as has the active part played by libraries as buyers of contemporary literature, along with the reviewing space available for new work. The internet, publishing on demand, social media, creative writing courses, networking and the celebrity culture have all been elements of revolution. Their blessings may be mixed, but by no means all the consequences have been negative. In addition to new possibilities for publishing and marketing, the kind of interest in the handmade typified by William Morris and the Kelmscott Press (much admired by Stephen Stuart-Smith) may be reviving, in the face of kindle and e-books, with a new awareness of the book as beautiful object. And the internet is at least partly responsible for the fact that unsolicited submissions to the Press, running at 20 or so a week in their heyday, have given way, as Stephen Stuart-Smith notes, to fewer, more informed and considered proposals.

Beyond the vagaries of fashion, and however modified over time, Enitharmon's commitment to the values represented by its founding spirits has been constant. But it is as true now as it was at the start that the funding of such an operation means the future is always likely to look precarious. Under both its Directors the Press has had the benefit of Arts Council funding, though this was halted for a time in 1985; and 2011 brought an end to regular three-year funding. A fund-raising auction was held in 1991, and a benefit reading in 2012; an Enitharmon Patrons and Friends scheme was set up. However, such initiatives cannot hope to replace regular core funding. Arts Council England funding came to an end in March 2017.

I would like to express my gratitude to Stephen Stuart-Smith and Isabel Brittain at Enitharmon for their help and encouragement, as well as for giving me the opportunity to read such a memorable body of work. Thanks are also due to Joanne Fitton, Head of Special Collections at the Brotherton Library, University of Leeds, where the Enitharmon archive is housed, to Danielle Dyal for her scrupulous, sharp-eyed checking of the typescript, and to Kathryn McCandless, for her help with the placing of the illustrations.

Finally – and crucially – many thanks to all the writers, translators and artists who have agreed to the inclusion of their work in this anthology.

LAWRENCE SAIL

David Jones, headpiece from *The Ancient Mariner* (2006)

# Contents

*An asterisk following a title indicates an entry in the Notes (pages 369 to 371)*

## POETRY

# PROSE

# List of Illustrations

*The illustrations in the colour sections and on the text pages have been selected by Lawrence Sail and Stephen Stuart-Smith. Full details are captioned in the places they appear.*

Front endpaper: Left: Norman Ackroyd, dust-jacket of Kevin Crossley-Holland's *Moored Man* (2006). Right: Peter Blake, watercolour of Dylan Thomas on the cover of *Under Milk Wood* (2014)

## *Starting Pistol*

Drawn into itself
a word is a thin

shaft of vision
that narrows

its shoulders
to aim

dead straight
for the hills.

But in the hope
of finding you

in deep focus
in front of me

standing arms out
where I can see you plainly

your dimensions
framed and discrete

I am trying to
hold back the long

discursive lines
from flying out

from racing after
one another in paler

and paler sequence.
I am trying to

string out
on my breath

certain floating words
before I find

they've disappeared
beyond earshot

into the quick
past tense of go.


*THE LIKENESS, 2014*

ALAN BROWNJOHN

## *Love / Poem*

Among the things I am mostly happy doing,
One needs a white page, another requires a white sheet.

The work on the white page demands ideas.
For the white sheet a suitable word might be dreams.

A great German poet once wrote that he counted beats
On the back of a beloved between white sheets.

One concluded that only genius could blend
The two distinct purposes in such a style,

Since mainly the two remain wholly separate,
And a difficult choice requires to be made:

Those in favour of the white page, please raise their hands . . .
Those in favour of the white sheets, please do the same . . .

Abstentions?

*A BOTTLE AND OTHER POEMS, 2015*

NANCY CAMPBELL

## Oqqersuut / The Message

Since I can't post a letter this far north,
I'm sending you an Arctic snowstorm,
the worst weather London's ever known:
deep drifts resisting shovel, salt and thaw.

Since I can't touch your winter skin
I appoint the most delicate snowflakes
to fall into your arms, kiss your cold face
and silence the city I loved you in.

I can't judge your heart's temperature,
although I lay out the last glacier
over the miles between us. Don't you hear
the wind? It calls to know your nature.

It's warmer than you think, for I have dressed
that wild inquisitor in my own breath.

*DISKO BAY, 2015*

## Walking on Water

The first ragged frill
round the fringe of the lake
tinny and splintering before
you put half your weight on it.

The waterway itself
was still mulberry and slate,
it hadn't even started
to straiten round the dogged barges.

Ice-houses, lantern-bright,
and white hoods nosing out to them,
snowmobiles cutting
huge figures of eight:
all weeks and weeks ahead.

Yet this was the first
of the season's mysteries:
'Winter must come,
the pale sun will stand still.
Nothing we do or say,
no prayers our old mothers pray,
can quicken or avert it.'

Meeting, dry-mouthed,
at the water's edge,
breathless we talked too much,
we were so careful not to touch,
and stared aghast at each other.

In the blue hour
a flutter of snow
– no more than a dozen flakes or so –
the first November birds.

Then winter came where we stood:
teeth, traps, and fierce forecasts,
death-mists, sudden shinings.
But still we looked, still
we stared: the worst
of winter burned away
and it became so clear.

I could see the two of us
way out from this beginning;
in your gaze I saw us both
in our summer season,
hands linked, love-locked,
walking on open water.


THE LANGUAGE OF YES, 1996

RHIAN GALLAGHER

## Nora Reading

She has removed herself as one who reads
removes under a lamp's glow.
Night of her hair, her highlighted cheek
as she leans into the story, her feet drawn up.

Yes, I am watching and listening.
The quiet that is never truly quiet,
close lives and streets,
a helicopter's tracking blades
above, beyond.

The room could be her room
in New York as here in London.
The interior is our discovery
and with discovery comes the desire
to hold it all in place.
This ease of being with her, that is all
and all and all.

*SHIFT, 2012*

U.A. FANTHORPE

## *Idyll*

Not knowing even that we're on the way,
Until suddenly we're there. How shall we know?

There will be blackbirds, in a late March evening,
Blur of woodsmoke, whisky in grand glasses,

A poem of yours, waiting to be read; and one of mine;
A reflective bitch, a cat materialised

On a knee. All fears of present and future
Will be over, all guilts forgiven.

Maybe, heaven. Or maybe
We can get so far in this world. I'll believe we can.

FROM ME TO YOU, 2007 *in association with Peterloo Poets*

PAUL MULDOON

## Till I Met You

Till I met you
I was a flag without a pole
A scrawl without a scroll
A soloist without a cue
A gadfly-sting without a herd
A thing without a word
Till I met you

Till I met you
I was a bird without a perch
A larch without a lurch
A merchantman without a crew
A butterfly without a jar
A sky without a star
Till I met you

There was a sense of something unfulfilled
When I decided to leave
As if we both still
Desperately wanted to believe

Till I met you
I was a scar without a scab
A jape without a jab
A labyrinth without a clew
A bellyful without a bag
A bull without a rag
Till I met you

*SONGS AND SONNETS, 2012*

MARIANNE MORRIS

## You Poem

you (walking up the road)
you, you (bird with a hole in its wing)
you you you (thought under pressure)
you you (didn't see what I was) you you you
(now see what I was) you you (a space
opening up between me and myself)
you you (a breath I took through being alone)
you you you (thought reduced to doubling) you
(blatant reformulation of) you you you (and me,
me, reformulating) you (a praxis) you (not
singing exactly) you you (can be forgiven for
everything) you (absolutely everything) you
(draw the lines according to what) you
(forgive, arrive late to the games) you
(a staging of battles) you you (just wanting more)
you you (of a nonspecific bounty) you you
(more and then less of me) you (music rising)
you you (up the stairs my thoughts climb)
you you (impose a structure onto the impossible)
you you (eternal suspension)


THE ON ALL SAID THINGS MORATORIUM, 2013

RHIAN GALLAGHER

*You*


Who could caress the core,
not founder at its coming,
nightmare with bindings all removed.

Be there for each, be each the other
who made it safe

to speak for the wordless one,
turn innocent ill-gotten shade.

With a touch to wake, a latent bruise,
living ghosts abroad come back.

Sister, friend, lover, much
was misgiven but tenderness
found us also, not always
at a loss; not always unloved, unlovable.


*SHIFT, 2012*

YANNIS RITSOS *versions by* DAVID HARSENT

## Don't Ask

It might be a nightclub logo
laying highlights on the pavement after rain,
or the sound of a cistern spilling,

or the silky splash
of a raindrop striking a rose, or you might decide
on the dark-out-of-darkness sob of a nightingale . . .

I glanced across and noticed how she slept
with her knee tucked up
and knew what I felt wasn't love, although, somehow,

the moment held all there was of tenderness:
the smell of the sheet, the fold of her knee, the fold
of the coverlet, that this was a warm evening in spring.

Look, who can say what these things mean?
They make patterns in our lives and all I know
is not knowing helps, but I couldn't tell you why.

*IN SECRET, 2012*

GREGORY WARREN WILSON

## The Point, the Turning

Each night you turn away from me to sleep,
as if sleep were some intimacy you felt
more privately than anything you feel for me.

We share the dark, this quilt, occasional dreams,
but on the point of sleeping you turn
modest, it seems, your back towards me

and in that moment leave me feeling
– not solitary, exactly, but . . . unconsoled.
I have my strategies: catch you, once you've fallen,

in an embrace you don't reciprocate, and breathe
your vanilla breath, an essence I now know
as well as this spine which comes between us

embodying what can never be said; self-evident
as a warm fossil embedded in the sheets;
or a history in Braille – syllables of bone

legible only because you trust me enough
to turn your back on me, turning alone
into the unintelligible night.

*JEOPARDY, 2003*

PIERRE JEAN JOUVE *translated by* DAVID GASCOYNE

from *MATIÈRE CÉLESTE*
*Hélène*

## A Lone Woman Asleep | Une seule femme endormie

When there came days sunk deep in damp your beauty seemed increased
And ever warmer grew your glow when rain fell in despair
And when days came that were like deserts you
Grew moister than the trees in the aquarium of time
And when the ugly anger of the world raged in our hearts
And sadness lisped exhausted through the leaves
You became as sweet as death
Sweet as teeth in the ivory skull-box of the dead
And pure as the skein of blood
Your laughter made to trickle down from your soul's parted lips
When there come days deep-sunk and damp the world grows still more dark
When days like deserts come, the heart is drenched with tears.


*DESPAIR HAS WINGS: SELECTED POEMS, ed. Roger Scott, 2007*

DUNCAN FORBES

## Vision Mixer

Abracadabra.  Magic wand.
Please read my thought waves and respond.

You know my number.  Ring me now.
Surprise yourself and break a vow.

Distressed, possessed, *id est* obsessed,
I have this passionate request.

I want you now.  I want you here.
I want you in my egosphere.

I'm willing you to drive this way.
Telepathy.  I hope and pray.

Drop everything.  Get in the car.
Accelerate.  Come as you are.

Without you time goes oh so slow
North of despair and east of woe.

Tonight began more years ago
Than I would ever let you know.

*VOICE MAIL, 2002*

FEDERICO GARCÍA LORCA

*translated by* JANE DURAN *and* GLORIA GARCÍA LORCA

## The Unfaithful Wife

And so I took her to the river
thinking she was a maiden,
but she had a husband.

It was the night of Santiago
and almost honour-bound.
The streetlamps went out
and the crickets lit up.
In the last streetcorners
I touched her sleeping breasts
and they opened for me suddenly
like bunches of hyacinths.
The starch of her petticoat
made a sound in my ears
like a piece of silk
slit by ten knives.
With no silver light in their branches,
the trees have grown,
and a horizon of dogs
barks far from the river.

•

Out past the brambles,
the reeds and the hawthorns,
under her mane of hair
I dug a hole in the silt.
I took off my tie.
She took off her dress.

I, my belt and revolver.
She, her four bodices.
Neither tuberose nor sea-conch
has such fine skin,
nor do crystals with moonlight
shine with such brilliance.
Her thighs escaped me
like startled fish,
half-filled with fire,
half-filled with cold.
That night I ran
the best of all roads, mounted
on a mother-of-pearl filly,
no bridle and no stirrups.
As a man, I will not say
the things she said to me.
The light of understanding
has made me restrained.
I carried her from the river,
dirty with sand and kisses.
The irises were beating
the air with their spears.

I behaved as who I am.
As a true gypsy.
I gave her a large sewing basket
of straw-yellow satin,
and I did not want to fall in love
because, having a husband
she told me she was a maiden
when I took her to the river.

*GYPSY BALLADS, 2011*

SHARON MORRIS

## The Will of the Heart

A plate of fish baked in salt,
lubina, pez espada, atún, lenguado –
we lift the skin from the white of fish,
part flesh from bone.

Last night we saw the trawlers out
at sea in the deepening wind.

In this village of fishermen,
La Isleta del Moro,
every front door bears a plaque –
María del Carmen,
The Sacred Heart,
Our Lady of Sorrows,
Virgin of the Sea.

At the table behind you he is talking
into a mobile phone,
tears in his eyes,
stretching fingers out wide
then clutching his fist to his heart –
'mi corazón … mi corazón'.


FALSE SPRING, 2007

SEBASTIAN BARKER

## A Week in the Country

Soon we must be leaving.
   The pink sheets are folded
On the bed we may never see again.

The crocus in the barrel by the front door
   Breathes a yellow so radiant
We shall remember it

Long after the candlelit dinners,
   And what we said, are forgotten.
And surely, too, the robin,

Proud in his livery on the back lawn
   Under the pine trees, will brighten
The dark shadows which fall on our past.

So, until we leave, let us be living
   And loving, that our regret may be so intense
Happiness follows us like a faithful dog.


*THE HAND IN THE WELL, 1996*

MICHAEL LONGLEY

## The Linen Industry

Pulling up flax after the blue flowers have fallen
And laying our handfuls in the peaty water
To rot those grasses to the bone, or building stooks
That recall the skirts of an invisible dancer,

We become a part of the linen industry
And follow its processes to the grubby town
Where fields are compacted into window-boxes
And there is little room among the big machines.

But even in our attic under the skylight
We make love on a bleach green, the whole meadow
Draped with material turning white in the sun
As though snow reluctant to melt were our attire.

What's passion but a battering of stubborn stalks,
Then a gentle combing out of fibres like hair
And a weaving of these into christening robes,
Into garments for a marriage or funeral?

Since it's like a bereavement once the labour's done
To find ourselves last workers in a dying trade,
Let flax be our matchmaker, our undertaker,
The provider of sheets for whatever the bed –

And be shy of your breasts in the presence of death,
Say that you look more beautiful in linen
Wearing white petticoats, the bow on your bodice
A butterfly attending the embroidered flowers.

*THE ROPE-MAKERS, 2005*

CHRISTOPHER REID

## *The Language of Love*

1

*Mon poux,*
contraction of *mon époux:*
endearment.
Louse for spouse!
From the topsy-turvy
language of love.
*Mon p'tit poux:*
the two *ps* making
a quickfire double kiss.
Thank you. Thank you.

2

*Tu es une ange!*
But *ange* is masculine
and you loved French too much
to let me get away
with such a solecism.
So I repeated it often,
as I do today
addressing you,
unmasculine angel!

ANNIVERSARY, 2015

THOM GUNN

## Coffee Shop

I recognize them in the booth,
Weak, greedy, lovely in their greed,
Shakily locking mouth to mouth,
Where mutually they start to feed.

The first kiss prelude to a tale
Where neither entertains suspicion
How they might change, how they might fail.
Nothing can shake this recognition:

The moment that they break into
The closed-up house of love; they slip
From room to room and, as they do,
Adventure through a companionship

Thick with their projects. What is best,
They know they'll not be bored again,
Proud to return the interest
They get and think they can sustain.

They drag the stocky shutters apart
And let light in upon the floor,
The dance-ground of the active heart,
Where they could play for ever more,

The lovers tangled in mid-phrase,
As if obstructed tongues might say:
'We are the same in different ways,
We are different in the same way.'

IN THE TWILIGHT SLOT, 1995

KATHLEEN RAINE

## Maire Macrae's Song

The singer is old and has forgotten
Her girlhood's grief for the young soldier
Who sailed away across the ocean,
Love's brief joy and lonely sorrow:
The song is older than the singer.

The song is older than the singer
Shaped by the love and the long waiting
Of women dead and long forgotten
Who sang before remembered time
To teach the unbroken heart its sorrow.

The girl who waits for her young soldier
Learns from the cadence of a song
How deep her love, how long the waiting.
Sorrow is older than the heart,
Already old when love is young:
The song is older than the sorrow.

*THE OVAL PORTRAIT AND OTHER POEMS, 1977*

JOHN MOLE

## Farewell, My Lovely

*A film noir ballad*


I was yours and you were mine
around the block, straight down the line,
but, honey, it's just too close to call
now that the writing's on the wall.

I've split and thrown away the key,
undoubled our indemnity.
What we had was once white hot
but passion cools in a tight spot.

The friendly cop who just dropped by
to chew the fat and apple pie
had something other on his mind.
Both of us know what he could find.

The beach house where we spent that night
sleeps in the moon's adulterous light.
Guilty, shameless, unafraid,
we laid our plans and then got laid.

Tomorrow is another day
and I'm a thousand miles away.
Distance fixes a broken heart.
Death is the car that will not start.

There were thoughts we dared not think
when we fixed your husband's drink.
So that's my story, more or less,
though you'll be telling yours, I guess.

You said I was a heel. I am.
Together we fixed the insurance scam,
both of us in it for the ride,
but our goose is cooked, the fish are fried.

The phonograph plays *Tangerine*.
Life is an empty coke machine.
Your ankle bracelet haunts me still.
If that can't save us nothing will.


*THE POINT OF LOSS, 2011*

KESTON SUTHERLAND

## Extreme Sweet

When did our joint faction against each
other split into this mess, cast about
every day for answers to that sex
question riveting us to indifference.
Your peculiarity reduced. Thick with
sex-knots a scab of hair clapped you on.

Passengers on the London train out
the window gravel and paint
tired. Sex is disclosed you took
up the converted hamper flipping
its pointless lock open. I can't sit
and long desperately for you alone.

Instead of ropes the descent in
autumn from the trees belongs
to leaves agitated by our rapacity,
by any exit. Throw your legs open.
Heartless blood in the wind, thin
spaced eyelashes and cars,

tossed there and all glassier than bat
breath on your mirror. It figures that
we fail and come out of it sex
first through the collided, straight
edged coalescence of sanity and
wait alone. There are other ways.

POETICAL WORKS, 1999–2015, 2015

SUE HUBBARD

## I dreamt I remembered what love was

For one fraudulent moment,
with your lips on my hardening breast,
our bodies strange in the darkness
pressed close in the promise of that narrow bed –
our alien selves,
our fears,
shed momentarily,
hung up on the hook behind the door,
I dreamt I remembered what love was.

Bound together by darkness,
unfamiliar limb exploring
unfamiliar limb in
temporary tenderness,
the soft dawn rain outside
my hair tumbling like a cliché on your chest,
I dreamt I remembered what love was.

*EVERYTHING BEGINS WITH THE SKIN, 1994*

DAVID JONES

## Prothalamion*

*for M & H*


At the time of the dooms
in the third quarter of the Reaper's Moon,
in the Island of Britain, in Troy Novaunt,
at the approach of the hateful and evil decision
at about the inception of the last round, toward
the time of the ultimate uncovering—when the
speaking is of no further consequence and naked
mechanism decides who shall be master.

In flame-lap and split masonry,
where the high fires leap and the merchandise
of the merchants, under whatsoever deep
vaulting, rocks now, knows the blast, feels the
unpredictable violence. When the poor, in
ramshackle habitation or flimsy bunk-hole,
apprehend in their innocent bodies horrors
unnamed from the foundation of the world.
When Troy towers are a feeble analogy and
the Harrying of the North a child's tale, when
fear rules and bombast pretends to competence.
Because of the detestable counsel, directly
because of the merchants' rule. When there is
hurrying in the streets (these dive where the
architrave juts—or under any appearance of
cover). At the time of the howling, in the days
of the final desolations, at the precise moment
of the eclipse:
Margaret (gentle as falcon, or
hawk of the tower) with

Harman, my sweet friend
spread in a vault their bed of unity, to mock
the unmaking.

  So have I heard bird-song, beneath the
trajectory zone, at Passchendaele, or seen
flowers lean toward each other, under the sun
that shined to delineate the hate and mutilation
of the Forward Area.

WEDDING POEMS, *ed. Thomas Dilworth,* 2002

David Jones, *The Bride,* wood engraving of 1930 from the
dust-jacket of *Wedding Poems* (2002)

SEAMUS HEANEY

# from *The Testament of Cresseid**

A gloomy time, a poem full of hurt
Should correspond and be equivalent.
Just so it was when I began my work
On this re-telling, and the weather went
From close to frosty, as Aries, mid-Lent,
Made showers of hail from the north descend
In a great cold I barely could withstand.

Still, there I stood, inside my oratory
When Titan had withdrawn his beams of light
And draped and sealed the brightness of the day,
And lovely Venus, beauty of the night,
Had risen up and toward the true west set
Her golden face, direct in opposition
To the god Phoebus, straight descending down.

Beyond the glass her beams broke out so fair
I could see away on every side of me.
The northern wind had purified the air
And hunted the cloud-cover off the sky.
The frost froze hard, the blast came bitterly
From the pole-star, whistling loud and shrill,
And forced me to remove against my will.

I had placed my trust in Venus, as love's queen
To whom one time I vowed obedience,
That she should sprig my fallow heart with green;
And there and then, with humble reverence,
I thought to pray her high magnificence,
But hindered by that freezing arctic air
Returned into my chamber to the fire.

Though love is hot, yet in an older man
It kindles not so soon as in the young:
Their blood turns furiously in every vein
But in the old the blaze is lapsed so long
It needs an outer fire to burn and bring
The spark to life – as I myself know well:
Remedies, when the urge dies, can avail.

I stacked the fire and got warm at the hearth,
Then took a drink to soothe and lift my spirit
And arm myself against the bitter north.
To pass the time and kill the winter night
I chose a book – and was soon absorbed in it –
Written by Chaucer, the great, the glorious,
About fair Cresseid and worthy Troilus.

And there I found that after Diomede
Had won that lady in her radiance
Troilus was driven nearly mad
And wept sore and lost colour and then, once
He had despaired his fill, would recommence
As memory and hope revived again.
Thus whiles he lived in joy and whiles in pain.


*THE TESTAMENT OF CRESSEID, 2004*

TED HUGHES

# from *Venus and Adonis**

Venus, afloat on swansdown in the high blue,
Still far short of Paphos, felt the shock-wave
Of the death-agony of Adonis.

She banked and diving steeply down through cirrus
Sighted her darling boy where he sprawled
Wallowing in a mire of gluey scarlet.

She leapt to the earth, ripping her garment open.
She clawed her hair and gouged her breasts with her nails.
Pressing her wounds to his wounds as she clasped him

And screaming at the Fates: 'You hags shall not
Have it all your way. O Adonis,
Your monument shall stand as long as the sun.

The circling year itself shall be your mourner.
Your blood shall bloom immortal in a flower.
Persephone preserved a girl's life

And fragrance in pale mint. I shall not do less.'
Into the mangled Adonis she now dripped nectar.
His blood began to seethe – as bubbles thickly

Bulge out of hot mud. Within the hour
Where he had lain a flower stood – bright-blooded
As those beads packed in the hard rind

Of a pomegranate.  This flower's life is brief.
Its petals cling so weakly, so ready to fall
Under the first light wind that kisses it,

We call it 'windflower'.


SHAKESPEARE'S OVID, MCMXCV

NEIL CURRY

## from *The Bending of the Bow**

When Poseidon, the god
of the sea, goes after a well-built ship with wind
    and wave; smashes it, and sinks it, and drowns
almost the entire crew, you can imagine
    how happy the survivors are as they
struggle through the surf, caked with brine, and finally
    scramble up the beach –

                        well Penelope
was every bit as happy as that.  Her white arms
    were round his neck and she would not let go.


'But the gods haven't finished with us yet,' he said.
    'Old Teiresias warned me when I went
down to the House of the Dead to find out how
    I would get home. But no more of that.  It's late
and time for bed.'


                    'Your bed is waiting for you, but,'
    said Penelope, 'something must have put
a thought as dark as that into your mind.  What is it?
    Tell me about it.  Now.'


                        'What a woman!
Well then,' Odysseus said, 'you'll only drag it
    out of me, so I'll tell you.  We'll have no
secrets from one another.  But I warn you, it's
    a curious story.
                    Teiresias
told me that I must travel about through the world
    of men, carrying an oar in my hands,

till I come to a place whose people know nothing
    of the sea; eat no salt; and have never
seen a ship, its purple sails, or the long oars
    that drive them.  And there will be this sign:
a traveller will pass me on the road and say,
    "Is that a winnowing-fan you've got there
on your shoulder?"  There and then, on that very spot,
    I am to thrust the oar into the ground
and make an offering to Poseidon: a ram,
    and a bull and a boar.  And then I am
to come back home again and make sacrifices
    to all the immortal gods of heaven
in their due order.
                    Death will then come upon me
  in my old age, like a soft wind from the sea,
he said, and with all my family around me.'


 'Blessed be the gods,' said Penelope,
'if it is their will to guard you from more trouble.'


      They sat and talked.


                  Meanwhile Eurynome,
working by firelight, had put out soft blankets
      for them and laid bright coverlets upon the bed.

And then when all was ready, she led them to their room,
      to joy in the old ways of their love.


*THE BENDING OF THE BOW, 1993*

SHEILA WINGFIELD

## *Ilex*

Ilex: all shadows
Belong to your tree.

Your forbears grew
Beside high terror
Felt by Greeks
Also near Roman treachery.

The sacred oaks of Mamre
Known to Abraham
Rustled their leaves
In prophecy,
But ilex:
Yours rattle drily

As if from little fears
And doubts continually
Moving, hidden
In your dark centre

Or from some shame
That we recall
Painfully
In the night.

COLLECTED POEMS 1938–1983, 1983

MARTHA KAPOS

## The Blackberry

Your face is a cipher when your smile
splays out into the many

double directions a child takes on a walk,
twirling a stem of grass in an erratic

circle of two minds
*Do I want this? Do I want this?*

The smile on its way to your face
dawdles, lost in thought.

It is stopping to pick blackberries
on the hot path. The dangling

things on the verge of having
must hold still under the leaves.

Lift the berry slowly
between your thumb and forefinger

so it slips off whole from the stem,
all of its loose possibilities

you softly swallow intact in your mouth,
the round knob of syllables

making one word that sounds exactly right.
But its double kiss, thicketed and warm,

is a little white lie
cuffed in fur.  Hard losing itself

in soft, fusty and sweet, like hearing
your own voice all wrong.

Smash it like the toy you didn't want
against a wall.  If you could only

hold everything dark-coloured on your tongue
forever without breaking:

little reds becoming black
scripts written on your lips.


*MY NIGHTS IN CUPID'S PALACE, 2003*

JENNY JOSEPH

*Cherry*


Suddenly the cherry has opened.
I could believe it was love
Like the babe opening its eye.

Twig thickening on the air
Has become this burst of blossom.
It waves its appeal in the spring breezes;
O cherry, O open heart.


*NOTHING LIKE LOVE, 2009*

KATHLEEN RAINE

## Petal of White Rose

Petal of white rose
And rosy shell
Cast up by the tide:
Who can tell
This burnet sweetness
From memory,
From the deep sea
Record of a life
Shaped by the restless wave.

THE OVAL PORTRAIT AND OTHER POEMS, 1977
*in association with Hamish Hamilton*

JEREMY HOOKER

## Flints

They are ploughed out,
Or surface under surface

Washes away leaving the bleached
Floor of a sunken battleground.

Some are blue with the texture of resin,
The trap of a primeval shadow.

Others are green,
A relic of their origins.

The white one is
An eye closed on the fossil.

Worked in radial grooves
From the bulb of percussion

They shed brittle flakes.
The core with its brutal edge

Shaped the hand.

*SOLILOQUIES OF A CHALK GIANT, 1974*

SEAMUS HEANEY

## Holly

It rained when it should have snowed.
When we went to gather holly

the ditches were swimming, we were wet
to the knees, our hands were all jags

and water ran up our sleeves.
There should have been berries

but the sprigs we brought into the house
gleamed like smashed bottle-glass.

Now here I am, in a room that is decked
with the red-berried, waxy-leafed stuff,

and I almost forget what it's like
to be wet to the skin or longing for snow.

I reach for a book like a doubter
and want it to flare round my hand,

a black-letter bush, a glittering shield-wall
cutting as holly and ice.

LIGHT UNLOCKED: CHRISTMAS CARD POEMS,
ed. Kevin Crossley-Holland and Lawrence Sail, 2005

LUCY NEWLYN

*Conkers*


Peeled, their padded rinds
discarded like old jackets,
they shine smooth and clean

as ocean-polished shells,
perfect as castings
loosened from their moulds,

entire unto themselves
as fresh-baked loaves, or podded
peas, or just-laid eggs, or berries.

You turn them over like a familiar
tune or a remembered line,
stilled by their touch and gleam.

Cool and hard they lie,
each one ringed concentrically
like the cross-section of a tree

in fold on fold of marbled gold-
sienna-chestnut-red-mahogany,
their dark sheen luminous

and naked as an eye.


*EARTH'S ALMANAC, 2015*

MICHAEL FIELD

## Noon*

Full summer and at noon; from a waste bed
Convolvulus, musk-mallow, poppies spread
The triumph of the sunshine overhead.

Blue on refulgent ash-trees lies the heat;
It tingles on the hedge-rows; the young wheat
Sleeps, warm in golden verdure, at my feet.

The pale, sweet grasses of the hayfield blink;
The heath-moors, as the bees of honey drink,
Suck the deep bosom of the day.  To think

Of all that beauty by the light defined
None shares my vision!  Sharply on my mind
Presses the sorrow: fern and flower are blind.

WINGED WORDS: VICTORIAN WOMEN'S POETRY AND VERSE,
ed. Catherine Reilly, 1994

JEAN MAMBRINO *translated by* KATHLEEN RAINE

## Sense

Rain refreshes the shadows,
makes the points of the leaves glitter,
as the sun threads its way
between the drops.  Earth perfumes itself
afresh, takes on the colour
of the gilded sunset.
Catch this moment to offer it,
consecrate it.  For the mind
effaces scents from memory,
which reflects only the meaning
of what was offered you,
the prayer of what is over.

*LAND OF EVENING, 2004*

SIMON ARMITAGE

## Dew*

The tense stand-off
of summer's end,
the touchy fuse-wire
of parched grass,
tapers of bulrush and reed,
any tree
a primed mortar
of tinder, one spark
enough to trigger
a march on the moor
by ranks of flame.

Dew enters the field
under cover of night,
tending the weary and sapped,
lifting its thimble of drink
to the lips of a leaf,
to the stoat's tongue,
trimming a length of barbed-wire fence
with liquid gems, here
where bog-cotton
flags its surrender
or carries its torch
for the rain.

Then dawn, when sunrise
plants its fire-star
in each drop, ignites
each trembling eye.

STANZA STONES, 2013

68

RAYNE MACKINNON

## from *The Blasting of Billy P.*

                Next Tuesday was the date
When Purvis saw the board; it was midday;
Young Alec had been sent a model kit
But could make nothing of it. 'Crikey, how
Do all the parts fit in? I'll never make
A model of the Bismarck at this rate.'
The ward was stale with boredom, but just then
A bell rang, and it flicked the atmosphere
Open. 'That's Purvis back,' said Tom; it was.
'Whit did ah tell you?' shouted Bill P.,
'Ah'm getting a complete discharge. Ye'll no
Call me an idiot the noo. Ah put
All ma cards down on the table.' 'Good for you,'
Said Tom, 'send us a postcard when yer clear.'
'Ah ye can laugh,' said Purvis, 'but it's true;
Anither week and ah'll be clear of here.'
'Dinna drink too much whisky,' said old Jock.
'Ah'll no dae that. Ah'm a good-living man,
Ah'm staying with ma sister, so I am.
But noo ah'll hev tae go and see the charge,
Ah've plenty tae sort oot.'

                A week went by
And Billy's blast-off came. His bony frame
Poked through a new brown suit, just like old wine
In a new wineskin. 'How'll ye pass the time?'
Asked Tom. Then Purvis sighed. 'Ah cannae get
A job. Ah've wasted ma best years in here.
Ah haevne seen ma sister fur ten year.'
'Ach cheer up, Bill,' said Tom, 'yer getting oot

And that's the main thing.' 'Why did ah refuse
A local?' Purvis said, 'Ah could hev worked
Away in the garden all the day,
And got ma keep.' Just then a van pulled up
Before the block.  Bill went round shaking hands
With all the patients who were ill at ease.
'Ah'll no forget ye, boys,' he said, 'And we'll
Remember you Bill,' someone said, then sagged
Into silence. 'Come on, Bill,' said the charge,
'Yer friends are waiting up in Aberdeen,
They'll give ye a right welcome.' Purvis sniffed.
'That'll be right,' he said, went through the door
And out of their lives.  As we sat and talked
Of Billy Purvis and his ways, it seemed
His going left a silence and a space.


THE BLASTING OF BILLY P., 1978

VLADIMIR MAYAKOVSKY *translated by* HARRY GILONIS

## For British Workers
*(at the time of their General Strike)*


Stations stationary,

                 all in the docks docked.

Police up and about

                   doing their 'duty'.

We stand stock still, shiver

                      at every news report

Just as in the 10 Days

                that shook the year '17.

Radios rotate

           their steel necks;

they're listening.

             Listening

                 from across the Channel.

Will they overcome?

              Give in?

                Be betrayed?

Or greet us, join us, with (beautiful) red banners?

I can hear,

         hear

               the troop-lorries rumbling . . .

The clank of weaponry . . .

                 The clink of spurs . . .

Into the docks

          go the black-legs.

Sea,

    into their apologies for faces

                   send a shit-storm!

I hear the trickle

           from piss-poor functionaries.

Ramsay Mac.

                making concessions

to Baldwin,

            a Brit-Menshevik . . .

A bolt from the blue

            and all's washed up!

I hear

        weeping filling the silences.

Nothing to eat.

           Not even a tipple.

Pea-souper,

        thick and nutritious,

                   feed the strikers!

Let Rimbaud's stones

            become slogan bread!

Radio silence.

         The heavens have downed tools.

Empyrean,

       time

        to call a halt.

Earth,

    don't do

        a hand's

            turn.

British workers,

        stand your ground.

Don't get caught out

              by

                  soft-soap compromisers,

burn brilliantly,

        don't

           sputter –

Herewith

        fraternal greetings

           and a few *kopecks*,

a friendly hand
                    heart-felt.
Not political *charades* –
Bolsheviks
            don't do fairy-tales.
Your joy –
            is our joy,
your pain
            and misfortune
                        ours.
I'd like
        now
            to get a new job as a bird,
fly over to London and embrace you all,
all five million –
                    excuse my over-enthusiasm!
perhaps
        even a few
                (un-English) kisses . . .


*VOLODYA: SELECTED WORKS, ed. Rosy Carrick, 2015*

FRED D'AGUIAR

*Legal Tender*\*

1

I wait so long
I stand so still
Swallows sit on my
Shoulders and wash
In the fonts at my neck
I carry rain
Two cups' worth
In the dippers of my
Clavicles
I have no energy
To shoo them from me
One pecks something
From the stubble on my
Priced and purchased chin
I look old before my
Time while my time
Makes me look
Preternaturally
Older than I should be
Both are not the same
One is a set of lines
Chiselled in my forehead
The other curlicues
My spine and spirit
Spirit is the negative
In this picture of me
What I store in the crook
Of my arms where

The natural light
Plunges into darkness
I send from my time
To yours
I want to blink
I wish to roll my shoulders
Stretch my arms
Empty my clavicles
Of what's pooled there
More than a pulse
In my neck
Less than a breath
Touch my dry eyes
With your fingers
Dipped in free rain


2

Old man's head
Grafted to young
Underfed body

All skin and sharp
Bones and not
Much gristle

Polished skin
Refracts light
Sinews harbor

Shadows that
Define how this
Freed slave owns

Less than his
Owner's name
How his body

Looks as if
An increase
In daylight

Might crumble its
Papyrus into
Weightless ash

So that we see
Not this man
In this light

Not a freed slave
But the heads
Of our parents

Planted on the
Round shoulders
Of our children


3

As ordered
I wash with soap
History's soap

Hot on my skin
Onion skin
Crackles off me

Soap wraps gun-
Powder into balm
Binds sulphur

I wash off layers
Of black for what's
White underneath

Then raw red
Till I shine
Tin-whistle-clean

Whistle hollowed
From my whitened
Skin-and-bones

Play something


*I HAVE FOUND A SONG, 2010*

SEBASTIAN BARKER

## from *The Impenetrability of Silence*

VI

Poems shall nevermore exist, and prayer shall be housed in museums.

Saintly people will snap like twigs, and the future of personality will be all in the past.

Time will have ticked its bit, and the shape of space will have finally folded its volume.

Gravity will give up its demands, and the laws of aerodynamics will kneel immobile in stone.

Tortured aristocrats will cease to howl, and the nightingale shall twinkle forever in the ear and the eye of the torturer.

The printing-press will print wine, and the wine-press shall shoot forth a dry alphabet.

Sunsets shall be eradicated, and the miraculous emptiness of space shall throw off its last vestment of illusion.

The medium of all media will burn between galaxies, and the speeding spaceship shall seem like a paperboat on the Atlantic.

Tunnelling pot-holers shall emerge into daylight even as they touch pointblank rockface, and the librarian in the city vault shall enter the impenetrability of silence.

*GUARDING THE BORDER: SELECTED POEMS, 1992*

BENJAMIN ZEPHANIAH

## Neighbours

I am the type you are supposed to fear
Black and foreign
Big and dreadlocks
An uneducated grass eater.

I talk in tongues
I chant at night
I appear anywhere,
I sleep with lions
And when the moon gets me
I am a Wailer.

I am moving in
Next door to you
So you can get to know me,
You will see my shadow
In the bathroom window,
My aromas will occupy
Your space,
Our ball will be in your court.
How will you feel?

You should feel good
You have been chosen.

I am the type you are supposed to love
Dark and mysterious
Tall and natural
Thinking, tea total.
I talk in schools

I sing on TV
I am in the papers,
I keep cool cats

And when the sun is shining
I go Carnival.


LONDON IN POETRY AND PROSE,
ed. Anna Adams, 2003

STUART HENSON

*Riddle**

Grab the beast by the horns.
Wrestle it down the narrow streets
till you break its will
to skitter its own way.
Subdue it.  Burden its rib-cage.
Let your children ride.
And then let it stray.
Who cares?  They'll send
a herdsman to round it up
at the end of the day.

*THE NEW EXETER BOOK OF RIDDLES,*
*ed. Kevin Crossley-Holland and Lawrence Sail, 1999*

## Marianne Faithfull (2)

The sixties are a loop in the time-film,
pacifism, pot, a blazing decade
extended like a summer through dog-days
to a mellow shimmer.  They've gone away,

the ones who expected to change the world
in velvets, lace, the flower-children who sat
up all night with guitars.  They disappeared
or recycled themselves in the brain-fade

of too much acid.  All the kaftans, beads
were left behind as though a tribe had faced
extinction, and cleared off into the hills.
You were part of that damaged exodus,

one of the rejects hooked on methadone,
excess, smashing the glass to find yourself
without a face or torso.  Through the hole
are glass splinters, a blue pigmented wall.

And then that raw whiskey-burnt voice came through
with 'Broken English', concentrated pain
feeding each song, away back into life,
an affirmation that it could be done,

anger and re-birth redress the balance,
point the way to a continuity
for a blonde Billie Holiday; cracked timbre
evoking in part a Brecht cabaret

singer, someone leaning by a piano,
inhaling on a red-tipped cigarette,
feeling into a sad song and assured
despite the shadow, the plaintive regret.


*VOODOO EXCESS, 2015*

EDWIN BROCK

## Symbols of the Sixties

On a quiet Sunday
when the sun is out
you can drive to
a village in Kent
which boasts a
coffee bar with plastic
tables. Among the
paraphernalia on the
walls a bird in a
painted cage says
Ban the bomb ban
the bomb ban the
bomb ban the bomb.
Boys in shiny jackets
fidget there with
beehive girls. The chickens
look brittle and taste
as though they were made
in the same factory
as the tabletops.

*FIVE WAYS TO KILL A MAN: NEW AND
SELECTED POEMS, 1990*

HAROLD PINTER

## Death
*(Births and Deaths Registration Act 1953)*


Where was the dead body found?
Who found the dead body?
Was the dead body dead when found?
How was the dead body found?

Who was the dead body?

Who was the father or daughter or brother
Or uncle or sister or mother or son
Of the dead and abandoned body?

Was the body dead when abandoned?
Was the body abandoned?
By whom had it been abandoned?

Was the dead body naked or dressed for a journey?

What made you declare the dead body dead?
Did you declare the dead body dead?
How well did you know the dead body?
How did you know the dead body was dead?

Did you wash the dead body
Did you close both its eyes
Did you bury the body
Did you leave it abandoned
Did you kiss the dead body


THE DISAPPEARED AND OTHER POEMS, 2002

DUNCAN FORBES

## Memorandum for the Grand Panjandrum

Administrivia are more and more a matter
Of total imbuggerance to me as an enemy
Of futile form-filling and carcinogenic jargon.
Who gives an acronym for idiotic idiom,
The turgid verbiage of oligarch's dittography,
The upstart footnote and its vermiform appendix,
Minutes of minutiae, quandaries of questionnaires,
Pleonastic paperwork, labyrinths of legalese
And photocopulation? Are you a fellow-sufferer
In post-potato Europe of pre-proforma trauma?
It's the Year of the Friend and I'm looking for a pen-friend.

*TAKING LIBERTIES, 1993*

JUDY GAHAGAN

## Out of the Dark

Because your call comes out of the dark
uninhabited hours beyond the curfews
beyond the frontiers of my quotidian

because your call
comes out of the dark, unmarked hours
where exiles live
crosses the gulf between us

because your voice is slow
its inflections charismatic
I paint an iconostasis
of your remote country
the continuously falling snow of it
lit by candlelight.

I know your country's lost
as you are too.
Which one of your wandering selves
could be trusted?

My candles reach and sway
ludicrous and ecstatic
as the gypsy diva
colossal in red satin
singing the *cantec de mehale*
the songs of the outskirts
pouring out her vibrato
in a concrete shed
singing her falsetto:
'live passionately, live passionately.'

THE SECRET FRONTIERS, 2008

KAJAL AHMAD *translated by* MIMI KHALVATI
*and* CHOMAN HARDI

## Directions

Whenever he was in the mountains,
wherever he took off his shoes,
they would always point towards his city
but he never thought that this might mean
his homeland would be liberated.
Now that he's in his city,
wherever he leaves his shoes,
they point towards lands beyond his
but he never dreams that the day
might come when, without seeing
the mirage that exile always sees,
without any direction from his shoes,
he will travel through the heart of his country,
store myth in his grandmother's wooden chest
and, in the cellar of a happy house,
close many colourful doors on it
like the doors in his childhood stories.

POEMS, 2008 *in association with the Poetry Translation Centre*

MICHAEL SYMMONS ROBERTS

## Wireless

*(In May 1897, Marconi sent the first radio message across water, from Lavernock in South Wales, to Flat Holm in the Bristol Channel. The message was the letter 'S')*

'S', hiss, primal sound, default letter
from which all speech, music, books were born,
dot-dot-dot, morse for white noise.
The first trip radio made over water
carried as its luggage 'S'; waves across waves
it told the sea a story in its own voice,
a tale of water on a shingle beach.

*

In hyperspaces between stations,
radio reverts to sibilance, to 'S',
the universal broadcast of a plural.
Maybe Marconi was weaned on a word
made to be whispered – *sarsaparilla* –
dark juice of underground forced up
on a breath between palate and tongue.

*

'S' in morse without 'O' 'S'. Save, just
save – he was too uncertain of his soul.
Does radio have a half-life, weakening
as it loops and loops the world?
Somewhere in a dripping cave where wireless
goes to die, Marconi's 'S' curls like a paper
message washed out of its bottle.

*

Obsolete distress calls dumped by radio
waves in rock pools glow like ripe
cherry anemones.  I fished some out
and held against my ear the faded maydays,
tragic as Titanic luggage, unpacked
now by scientists, silk and lace falling
from their folds like shimmering spirits.

*

White roses as sensitive as crystal sets,
planted at the end of each row of vines.
If there's sickness in the air, roses will
fall first, and precious champagne grapes
are sprayed and netted.  So it was
with the earliest receivers.
They would catch a voice and die with it.

*

Marconi's voice: *sarsaparilla was my first,*
*waterglass my last, but I will keep*
*one more 'S' back, so when my tomb*
*is unsealed I will hiss*
*through parchment lips and then my face,*
*my origami death mask,*
*will be shocked to dust by open air.*

*

Wildtrack – radio with no voices, music,
codes, the sound of unmarked canvas.
At the end of each recording, thirty seconds'
nothing, a shared stillness. Actors,
audiences, engineers all honour it
because the dumb deserve a hearing,
and wireless always ends in silence.


*RADIO WAVES: POEMS CELEBRATING THE WIRELESS,*
*ed. Seán Street, 2004*

VERNON SCANNELL

## Hearing Aid

'Leopards pray,'
the surpliced voice intoned
from the Sunday morning radio.

The listener saw the furry creatures,
paws together, eyes half-closed,
a scene that William Blake might have composed.

On 'The World at One'
a different voice spoke of the need
for screaming pregnant women,

and the same listener saw
shrill images from Bosch or Fuseli
of female suffering and man's indifference.

Later in the day, on Radio 4,
a play was trailed: *Goats*, by Henry Gibson;
a bucolic comedy, no doubt.

And then the listener's wife
said, 'I've found it. Here. You left it in the loo,
as you so often do.'

Evening: Radio 3.
'The Great C Major', words now clear,
the image vivid, too:

tall, muscular and lean
in full dress uniform,
a stern, bemedalled Royal Marine.

*VIEWS AND DISTANCES, 2000*

JOHN HEATH-STUBBS

# Seventeen Hundred and Eighty-Nine
### (Bicentenary of Blake's Songs of Innocence)

The fortress fell – tyranny age-old,
Black ignorance, and cruelty, and injustice,
With the insolent levity that says to the starving
'Why can't you eat cake?'

That blissful morning of July, who might discern,
Beyond the bright, brave Phrygian cap,
A blood-stained blade descend –
Humane and rational machine of death?
The harlot of the abstract reason
Enthroned in the cathedral.
The lost traveller, the little boy lost,
Pursues a vapour still.

In Albion, in London's Golden Square
(Hovered above him quadrate golden Jerusalem),
A youthful craftsman, flaming-haired,
Corrodes with strong acid of revolution
The tablets of history, takes in hand
The honest tools of his trade, as he engraves
His songs and double images. He frames
The lamb in all its fearful symmetry,
Innocence of the tiger.

William Blake, towards Eternity
Ascending in Elijah's chariot – we know
The rose polluted by the secret worm,

Weariness of the sunflower;
And we have walked through every chartered street.

The vision of experience is ours.
You who guided Samuel Palmer's footsteps,
Where Virgil's shepherds pipe by Beulah's streams,
Show us once more the innocent vision: teach us
That, also, is valid.

*THE GAME OF LOVE AND DEATH, 1990*

MAUREEN DUFFY

## 60th Remembering: June 14th 2005

Beside the railway track the oxeye daisies
are open for business, the fireweed
tosses its willowy head whose small flames
once cauterised the wounds of the blitz.
Yet seared flesh and spirit still suppurate
under scar tissue letting out a thin seep of pain.
So my remembrance today is of my aunt
Ada, the clever one, on remission
from the airy sanatorium to convalesce
in our front room and, after the bomb fell
laid out on the cold pavement, as my mother
later told me.  Someone had given her
a wad of gauze that she dabbed at her wounded
forehead, unaware of the shattered legs below
and crying: 'Let me go with them.
I want to go with them.'

FAMILY VALUES, 2008

KATE RHODES

## Al-Musayyib, 16th July 2005

The houses are all the same,
low walls and shuttered windows.
Hard to imagine how the villagers survive –
scratching seeds into dust,
the desert singeing their heels.

Cars pass like seconds, never pausing.
The children are always busy,
boatbuilding from nothing
except rags and sticks and dreams,
sailing yachts across oceans of sand.

The bomb was planted before dawn,
blankets of shrapnel glittering on the road.
A soldier from Alabama was killed outright,
nothing left to send back home.
The defence say his friends stopped thinking.

They kicked down the schoolhouse door.
The children were completing a test
heads down, remembering the alphabet,
pencilled letters marching right to left
in neat, unfinished lines.

*THE ALICE TRAP, 2008*

MARIO PETRUCCI

## The Man Buried with Chernobyl

He's there.  You might even see him – if you look
hard with X-rays.  You could slice him like an embryo,

ply the great toothed wheel as it thrums with water – feed
cooling-water down the long shaft in an umbilical cord

of transparency, as though glass had come to life
twisting around steel.  Then stack each concrete wafer

to count it with Geigers: map his contours in roentgens,
reconstruct him in glowing 3D.  He might almost be

recognisable to his wife.  Perhaps he would stir – lift
from his calcined mould like a grit jelly.  Step off the VDU

imagining himself the corpse at the end of a play
leaving behind the murdered outline in white carbon.

HEAVY WATER: A POEM FOR CHERNOBYL, 2004

YANNIS RITSOS *versions by* DAVID HARSENT

## Women

Our women are distant, their sheets smell of goodnight.
They put bread on the table as a token of themselves.
It's then that we finally see we were at fault; we jump up saying,
'Look, you've done too much, take it easy, I'll light the lamp.'

She turns away with the striking of the match,
walking towards the kitchen, her face in shadow, her back
bent under the weight of so many dead –
those you both loved, those she loved, those
you alone loved . . . yes . . . and your death also.

Listen: the bare boards creaking where she goes.
Listen: the dishes weeping in the dishrack.
Listen: the train taking soldiers to the front.

*IN SECRET, 2012*

98

MICHAEL LONGLEY

## Bog Cotton

Let me make room for bog cotton, a desert flower –
Keith Douglas, I nearly repeat what you were saying
When you apostrophised the poppies of Flanders
And the death of poetry there: that was in Egypt
Among the sandy soldiers of another war.

(It hangs on by a thread, denser than thistledown,
Reluctant to fly, a weather vane that traces
The flow of cloud shadow over monotonous bog –
And useless too, though it might well bring to mind
The plumpness of pillows, the staunching of wounds,

Rags torn from a petticoat and soaked in water
And tied to the bushes around some holy well
As though to make a hospital of the landscape –
Cures and medicines as far as the horizon
Which nobody harvests except with the eye.)

You saw that beyond the thirstier desert flowers
There fell hundreds of thousands of poppy petals
Magnified to blood stains by the middle distance
Or through the still unfocused sights of a rifle –
And Isaac Rosenberg wore one behind his ear.

CENOTAPH OF SNOW, 2003

ISAAC ROSENBERG

## Break of Day in the Trenches*

The darkness crumbles away.
It is the same old druid Time as ever,
Only a live thing leaps my hand,
A queer sardonic rat,
As I pull the parapet's poppy
To stick behind my ear.
Droll rat, they would shoot you if they knew
Your cosmopolitan sympathies.
Now you have touched this English hand
You will do the same to a German
Soon, no doubt, if it be your pleasure
To cross the sleeping green between.
It seems you inwardly grin as you pass
Strong eyes, fine limbs, haughty athletes,
Less chanced than you for life,
Bonds to the whims of murder,
Sprawled in the bowels of the earth,
The torn fields of France.
What do you see in our eyes
At the shrieking iron and flame
Hurled through still heavens?
What quaver – what heart aghast?
Poppies whose roots are in man's veins
Drop, and are ever dropping;
But mine in my ear is safe –
Just a little white with the dust.

SELECTED POEMS AND LETTERS, ed. Jean Liddiard, 2003
in association with the European Jewish Publication Society

NEIL ASTLEY

## Listeners

'. . . he turned back to wave until the mist and the hill hid him . . . Panic seized me,
and I ran . . . to the top of the hill, and stood there a moment dumbly, with straining
eyes and ears. There was nothing but the mist and the snow and the silence of death.'
                                                              – Helen Thomas

And clattering down the iron-hard lane
(avoiding the ice), he'd halt at her voice
and hear only the rush of the silence;
a tinkle of couplings, way up the line.

There the broadcast ended, before Arras
where a shell-blast would stop his heart.
The sky outside looked utter black, I thought
(you had listened and were crying, for us,

across the city): one by one the lights
flicked out, as a plane's tail ember moved
through the darkness, unswerving, and silent.

You shivered that night in your cold sheets,
your window brushed by snow. I could hear
on my pane the same breathless whisper.

ELECTED FRIENDS: POEMS FOR AND ABOUT EDWARD THOMAS,
ed. Anne Harvey, 1991

MIKLÓS RADNÓTI

*translated by* GEORGE GÖMÖRI *and* CLIVE WILMER

## Your Right Hand under my Neck

I lay in bed last night, your right hand under my neck.
I asked you not to remove it – my day must still have been aching.
I listened at your wrist to the sound of the blood pulsating.

It was near midnight, and sleep had already flooded over me.
It broke on me suddenly – as long ago in the sleepy
Years of my downy childhood – and it rocked me just as gently.

It was not – so you tell me now – even three o'clock yet when
I started up in terror, and sat there – in my sleep
Mumbling, then declaiming, then screaming unintelligibly,

And I flung my arms out wide, as a bird ruffled with fear
Will beat its wings when a shadow sweeps the garden unpredictably.
Where was I heading?  Which way?  What form of death was it scared me?

You were there comforting me, and I let you, sitting asleep,
And lay back in silence, though still with the road of terrors ahead.
And went on dreaming.  Perhaps of some other death instead.

FORCED MARCH, 2003 *in association with the European Jewish
Publication Society*

MICHAEL HENRY

## Footnote to History

Something my cousin said,
some footnote to history
like the Christmas truce in World War One.
Some story about my uncle's minder
taking him for a drink
on their way back from the prison hospital.

But what amazed my cousin was
the German had unstrapped his gun-belt
and left it suspended from a hook.
Imagine the shadowy-lit interior
with its single bulb
like a moon three days shy of full,

the fug of fifty brands of smoke
pressing on the imprisoned air.
Imagine the double helix
from the cigarettes of friend and foe,
and the amber mugs of beer
shoulder to shoulder on the bar.

And hanging heavy in their cups,
the holstered guns at the edge
of the room.  At the edge of my uncle's eye.


FOOTNOTE TO HISTORY, 2001

## ISAAC ROSENBERG

### *August 1914*

What in our lives is burnt
In the fire of this?
The heart's dear granary?
The much we shall miss?

Three lives hath one life –
Iron, honey, gold.
The gold, the honey gone –
Left is the hard and cold.

Iron are our lives
Molten right through our youth.
A burnt space through ripe fields,
A fair mouth's broken tooth.

SELECTED POEMS AND LETTERS, ed. Jean Liddiard, 2003
in association with the European Jewish Publication Society

PETER REDGROVE

## Staines Waterworks

I

So it leaps from your taps like a fish
In its sixth and last purification
It is given a coiling motion
By the final rainbow-painted engines, which thunder;
The water is pumped free through these steel shells
Which are conched like the sea –
This is its release from the long train of events
Called *The Waterworks at Staines*.

II

Riverwater gross as gravy is filtered from
Its coarse detritus at the intake and piped
To the sedimentation plant like an Egyptian nightmare,
For it is a hall of twenty pyramids upside-down
Balanced on their points each holding two hundred and fifty
Thousand gallons making thus the alchemical sign
For water and the female triangle.

III

This reverberates like all the halls
With its engines like some moon rolling
And thundering underneath its floors, for in
This windowless hall of tides we do not see the moon.
Here the last solids fall into that sharp tip
For these twenty pyramids are decanters
And there are strong lights at their points
And when sufficient shadow has gathered the automata

Buttle their muddy jets like a river-milk
Out of the many teats of the water-sign.


IV

In the fourth stage this more spiritual water
Is forced through anthracite beds and treated with poison gas,
The verdant chlorine which does not kill it.


V

The habitation of water is a castle, it has turrets
And doors high enough for a mounted knight in armour
To rein in, flourishing his banner, sweating his water,
To gallop along this production line of process where
There are dials to be read as though the castle library-
Books were open on reading-stands at many pages –
But these are automata and the almost-empty halls echo
Emptiness as though you walked the water-conch;
There are very few people in attendance,
All are men and seem very austere
And resemble walking crests of water in their white coats,
Hair white and long in honourable service.


VI

Their cool halls are painted blue and green
Which is the colour of the river in former times,
Purer times, in its flowing rooms.

VII

The final test is a tank of rainbow trout,
The whole station depends on it;
If the fish live, the water is good water.


VIII

In its sixth and last purification
It is given a coiling motion
By vivid yellow and conch-shaped red engines,
This gallery like the broad inside of rainbows
Which rejoice in low thunder over the purification of water,

Trumpeting Staines water triumphantly from spinning conches to all taps.


*THAMES: AN ANTHOLOGY OF RIVER POEMS, ed. Anna Adams, 1999*

## U.A. FANTHORPE

## Rising Damp

( *for C.A.K. and R.K.M.*)

'A river can sometimes be diverted, but it is a very hard thing
to lose it altogether.'
    J. G. Head, paper read to the Auctioneers' Institute in 1907


At our feet they lie low,
The little fervent underground
Rivers of London

*Effra, Graveney, Falcon, Quaggy,*
*Wandle, Walbrook, Tyburn, Fleet*

Whose names are disfigured,
Frayed, effaced.

These are the Magogs that chewed the clay
To the basin that London nestles in.
These are the currents that chiselled the city,
That washed the clothes and turned the mills,
Where children drank and salmon swam
And wells were holy.

They have gone under.
Boxed, like the magician's assistant.
Buried alive in earth.
Forgotten, like the dead.

They return spectrally after heavy rain,
Confounding suburban gardens.  They infiltrate
Chronic bronchitis statistics.  A silken
Slur haunts dwellings by shrouded
Watercourses, and is taken
For the footing of the dead.

Being of our world, they will return
(Westbourne, caged at Sloane Square,
Will jack from his box),
Will deluge cellars, detonate manholes,
Plant effluent on our faces,
Sink the city.

*Effra, Graveney, Falcon, Quaggy,*
*Wandle, Walbrook, Tyburn, Fleet*

It is the other rivers that lie
Lower, that touch us only in dreams
That never surface.  We feel their tug
As a dowser's rod bends to the source below

*Phlegethon, Acheron, Lethe, Styx.*


THAMES: AN ANTHOLOGY OF RIVER POEMS,
ed. Anna Adams, 1999

BLAKE MORRISON

*Flood*

We live in the promise of miraculous lakes:
Dagenham, Greenwich, Wapping, the Isle of Dogs.

'When the siren sounds, those in the blue environs
Should proceed immediately to non-risk zones.'

Spring tides, high winds: for days we can hear
Of nothing else, our eyes bright with disaster,

Our dreams a chronicle of *mountaing anarchie,*
*The river-folke frantick, shippës trappt in trees.*

*And the dove we sent out, when it came back,*
*Had the brown glaze of estuaries on its beak.*

In our dreams no sandbags hold back the flood:
We would bring the whole world down if we could.


*PENDLE WITCHES, 1996*

MYRA SCHNEIDER

## The Carafe

drinks light
from the long windows,
is transfigured.

Below its tight neck
rounds more
than breast or belly.

Behind its glass wall
water has the tremble
of an uncertain mouth.

When it's tipped over
a tumbler, the choke
before the stream

is fear and anger
held for years,
breaking in my throat.

Release is walking
on rain-whitened grass
through curtains of sun.

*INSISTING ON YELLOW: NEW AND SELECTED POEMS, 2000*

ROGER MOULSON

## The Glass of Water

Amazed to find the thing it most desires
light strikes.
Glass rings around it.
The contents accept their shape
but do not own it
as if shape's the need to be held.
Water does not concern itself
which one holds
and which is held.
The glass stands on the ghost of itself.
It shines a beam through shadow
speaks of volume
of a single column.
Water waits to run.
It breathes into the mouth of air.
When it's most still
it is compelled towards the other always.

WAITING FOR THE NIGHT-ROWERS, 2006

CAROLE SATYAMURTI

## *Heartmarks*

This frail-looking balustrade,
all that stood between us and certain
death on the paving-stones below,
is where we first touched without
a spun glass reticence between us.

That Soho market . . . this revolving door . . .
the layout of the city is peppered
with such places.  To fix them
with precise coordinates of words
would arrest their gauzy meanings,

but on the map described by memory
you'll find me whirling nightly
from Bertaux to Pimlico, haunting
Long Acre, Kenwood, Gabriel's Wharf:
all the stations of love.

*LONDON IN POETRY AND PROSE, ed. Anna Adams, 2002*

DAVID GASCOYNE

## The Gravel-Pit Field

Beside the stolid opaque flow
Of rain-gorged Thames; beneath a thin
Layer of early evening light
Which seems to drift, a ragged veil,
Upon the chilly March air's tide:
Upwards in shallow shapeless tiers
A stretch of scurfy pock-marked waste
Sprawls laggardly its acres till
They touch a raw brick-villa'd rim.

Amidst this nondescript terrain
Haphazardly the gravel-pits'
Rough-hewn rust-coloured hollows yawn,
Their steep declivities away
From the field-surface dropping down
Towards the depths below where rain-
Water in turbid pools stagnates
Like scraps of sky decaying in
The sockets of a dead man's stare.

The shabby coat of coarse grass spread
Unevenly across the ruts
And humps of lumpy soil; the bits
Of stick and threads of straw; loose clumps
Of weeds with withered stalks and black
Tatters of leaf and scorched pods: all
These intertwined minutiae
Of Nature's humblest growths persist
In their endurance here like rock.

As with untold intensity
On the far edge of Being, where
Life's last faint forms begin to lose
Name and identity and fade
Away into the Void, endures
The final thin triumphant flame
Of all that's most despoiled and bare:
So these least stones, in the extreme
Of their abasement might appear

Like rare stones such as could have formed
A necklet worn by the dead queen
Of a great Pharoah, in her tomb . . .
So each abandoned snail-shell strewn
Among these blotched dock-leaves might seem
In the pure ray shed by the loss
Of all man-measured value, like
Some priceless pearl-enamelled toy
Cushioned on green silk under glass.

And who in solitude like this
Can say the unclean mongrel's bones
Which stick out, splintered, through the loose
Side of a gravel-pit, are not
The precious relics of some saint,
Perhaps miraculous?  Or that
The lettering on this Woodbine-
Packet's remains ought not to read:
*Mene mene tekel upharsin?*

Now a breeze gently breathes across
The wilderness's cryptic face;
The meagre grasses scarcely stir;
But when some stranger gust sweeps past,
Seeming as though an unseen swarm

Of sea-birds had disturbed the air
With their strong wings' wide stroke, a gleam
Of freshness hovers everywhere
About the field: and tall weeds shake,

Leaves wave their tiny flags to show
That the wind blown about the brow
Of this poor plot is nothing less
Than the great constant draught the speed
Of Earth's gyrations makes in Space . . .
As I stand musing, overhead
The zenith's stark light thrusts a ray
Down through the dusk's rolling vapours, casts
A last lucidity of day

Across the scene: and in a flash
Of insight I behold the field's
Apotheosis: No-man's-land
Between this world and the beyond,
Remote from men and yet more real
Than any human dwelling-place:
A tabernacle where one stands
As though within the empty space
Round which revolves the Sage's Wheel.

*SELECTED POEMS, 1994*

ALAN BROWNJOHN

## Doorway

Where it stood by the roadside, the frame for a view,
It made the step from one weed-patch to the next
A metaphor.  If I chose to walk across
This threshold to a mansion never built,
Could I manage to come back?  Having left the road
To stroll into the fields, I saw this lintel
Presenting its challenge.  And what it said was, *Walk*

*Through this door, you are going to walk through,*
*After which you will not be the same.*  I had thought,
Was I always on a journey to that place?
– And now, was I always travelling to where
I am to-night, by a fire toning down to grey
Its image in those glasses, beside the girl
Asleep in the opposite chair?  To such a stop?

To-night is six months onwards from that voice
Which said, *You have reached a stage where you must walk through,*
*And not expect to return to what you were.*
I am here because I turned back from that view,
Shaking my head and smiling, walking on
To where this girl smiles, in apparent sleep,
And stretches.  What she does first when she wakes

Is pick the glasses up, they suddenly
Shine scarlet from the curtains.  *What were you thinking?*
She says, as she goes past.  I shake my head,
And smile, watching the fire.  She goes on past
Its dying coil, then I realize she has stopped
And turned at the doorway behind me, tilting
The glasses in her hand.  And has said, *Walk through.*

THE SANER PLACES: SELECTED POEMS, 2011

C. DAY LEWIS

*The Gate*
*for Trekkie*


In the foreground, clots of cream-white flowers (meadowsweet?
Guelder?  Cow parsley?): a patch of green: then a gate
Dividing the green from a brown field; and beyond,
By steps of mustard and sainfoin-pink, the distance
Climbs right-handed away
Up to an olive hilltop and the sky.

The gate it is, dead-centre, ghost-amethyst-hued,
Fastens the whole together like a brooch.
It is all arranged, all there, for the gate's sake
Or for what may come through the gate.  But those white flowers,
Craning their necks, putting their heads together,
Like a crowd that holds itself back from surging forward,
Have their own point of balance – poised, it seems,
On the airy brink of whatever it is they await.

And I, gazing over their heads from outside the picture,
Question what we are waiting for: not summer –
Summer is here in charlock, grass and sainfoin.
A human event? – but there's no path to the gate,
Nor does it look as if it was meant to open.
The ghost of one who often came this way
When there was a path? I do not know.  But I think,
If I could go deep into the heart of the picture

From the flowers' point of view, all I would ask is
Not that the gate should open, but that it should
Stay there, holding the coloured folds together.
We expect nothing (the flowers might add), we only
Await: this pure awaiting –
It is the kind of worship we are taught.


SELECTED POEMS, *ed. Jill Balcon, 2004*

JON SILKIN

## Urban Grasses

With a sickle, I tended the dead in London
shortening the grass that had flowered
on their bodies, as it had in my child's.
And I piled the soil over the paupers' flesh
in their flimsy coffins, which split.  What else
was I to do?  It became
my trade, my living.

      *   *   *

Earth, I shall be unhappy to not know
how you go on, when I'm like those
I tended, shearing the grasses
above their foreheads.  I felt tenderness
yet I did not know them – and how should I re-assure
that nothing, and say, yes, I care for you
because you are nothing now.  Yet you are nothing.
Could I have dared tell them?
And therefore I remained silent.

LONDON IN POETRY AND PROSE, *ed. Anna Adams, 2002*

GERALD DAWE

## from *Déjà Vu*

In the squalls of rain before the sunlight came
along with a sudden gust up North Street and down by
discount shops and ragged car parks and the view all the way
to where we once lived like everyone else, or so we thought,
swimming in our own underworld with the Czech vase in the bay
window, the sun-blinds, the grandfather clock on the landing,
waking up in arctic bedrooms to milky skies and freezing mornings,
everyone heading to work, on packed buses –
could it have been so? – through autumn and winter,
spring and summer, women sitting on spruce porches
and steps in behind their front gardens and the kids
like a breed unto themselves, hanging out down the back
when the nights lengthened and you'd arrive in from
somewhere very different than this orderly world
that's gone now – like the pop of the gas-fire
being lit in granny's bedroom, the white columns
that turned sky-blue, the scraggy nights
of racing clouds, the kitchen lights going on,
one after another, at the same time, the shadows
on the ceiling, the songs of praise carrying on the wind,
the shining car parked where it shouldn't have been,
the sound of someone whistling down the lane
and the whole thing starting up all over again,
every morning without fail, come sun, rain or hail,
without you or I, without the blink of an eye.

*LOVE POET, CARPENTER: MICHAEL LONGLEY AT SEVENTY,*
*ed. Robin Robertson, 2009*

JACK KEROUAC

## from *Book of Haikus*


Barefoot by the sea,
    stopping to scratch one ankle
With one toe


                                        Barley soup in Scotland
                                            in November –
                                        Misery everywhere


Spring is coming
    Yep, all that equipment
For sighs


                                        Voices of critics
                                            in the theater lobby—
                                        A moth on the carpet


BOOK OF HAIKUS, 2004

BILLY COLLINS

## Lowell, Mass.


Kerouac was born in the same town
as my father, but my father never
had time to write *On the Road*

let alone drive around the country
in circles.

He wrote notes for the kitchen table
and a novel of checks
and a few speeches to lullaby
businessmen after a fat lunch

and some of his writing is within
me for I house catalogues of jokes
and handbooks of advice
on horses, snow tires, women,

along with some short stories
about the deadbeats at the office,
but he was quicker to pick up
a telephone than a pen.

Like Jack, he took a drink but
beatific to him meant the Virgin Mary.

He called jazz jungle music
and he would have told Neal Cassady
to let him off at the next light.


*THE APPLE THAT ASTONISHED PARIS, 2006*

ROBERT CREELEY

# from *Pictures*

1

This distance
between pane of glass,
eye's sight –
the far waving green edge

of trees, sun's
reflection, light
yellow – and sky there too
light blue.

3

*Harry's gone out for pizza.*
*Mabel's home all alone.*
*Mother just left for Ibiza.*
*Give the old man a bone?*

*Remember when Barkus was willing?*
*When onions grew on the lawn?*
*When airplanes cost just a shilling?*
*Where have the good times gone?*

5

Sun's shadows aslant
across opening expansive
various green fields down

from door
here ajar on box tower's
third floor –

look out on
wonder.
This morning.


*PICTURES, 2001*

TAMAR YOSELOFF

## Madison and 44th

Although it's been years, I can still describe
the way my first lover placed his hand on my knee,
what my mother served for dinner every night
the week my father and I didn't speak,
or how the light edged through the half-closed curtain
in my new home, a new country.
Is the bigger picture lost to me,

or is it there, shining in the silver helmet
of a phone kiosk collaged with dominatrix cards?
I had been hitting the big department stores
during January sales, pleased with my shiny bags
full of new clothes, trying to balance
the black receiver, the voice
at the other end, explaining gently.

On that corner, there will always be
pedestrians, taxis, dogs to be walked, shoppers like me.
The city may decide to move those phones,
they may be gone already for all I know.
Although your death can't come twice to me,
I will never stand there again,
stupid in my new shoes, fumbling for change.

BARNARD'S STAR, 2004

JEREMY REED

*Sunglasses*


The cool look, wide-screen Jackie O
blackouts in a circular frame,
eyewear like a tinted limo,

the car sealed like a mausoleum
flash outside Van Cleef & Arpels
for a laminated icon.

Jimmy Dean used shades as purdah,
thunder-black moodies airbrushing
a masochistic gay chutzpah.

Ray-Bans were a Warhol fetish,
industrial, alien wraparounds
glossy as raindropped nail polish.

They're image-props to attitude,
enigma, iris-free disdain,
staging a Rothko solitude

like Kirk's originals, amber
octagonals graduating to brown
lenses, as retro for an edgy star.

Mystique enhancers, Monroe-wear
to hide the bruises, or pushed up
as celeb pointers in the hair,

they're confirmation of a shift
away from centre, someone moved
into the corners, into foggy drift.

With some it's drugs, desperado
cover for altered states, the light
burning in, punishing as snow.

With others it's like a gated estate,
no point of contact tracking through the street
in aviators to meet a blonde date.


*PICCADILLY BONGO, 2010*

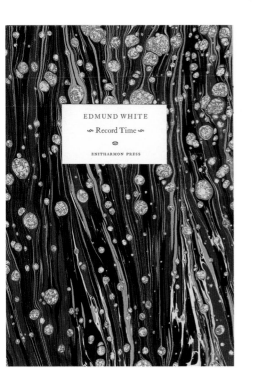

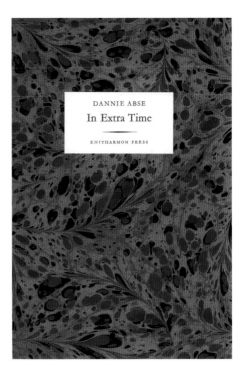

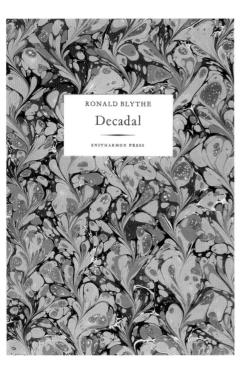

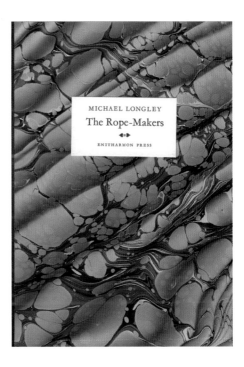

Marbled-wrappered letterpress-printed chapbooks

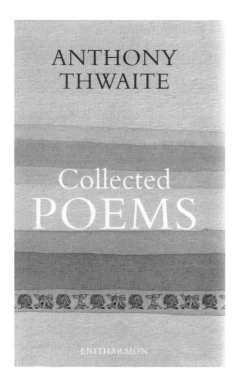

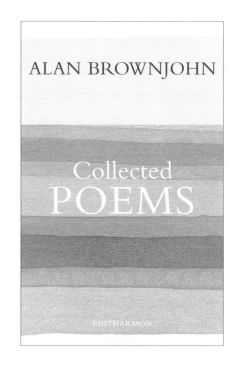

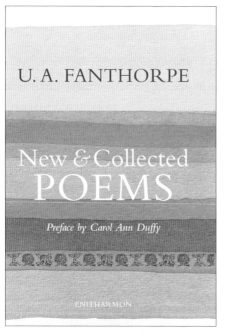

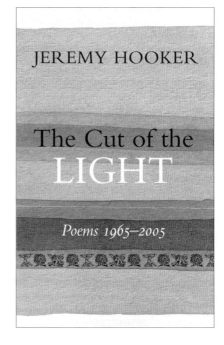

Series design for *Collected Poems*

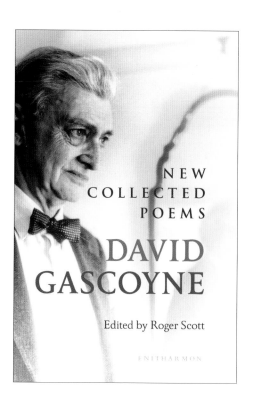

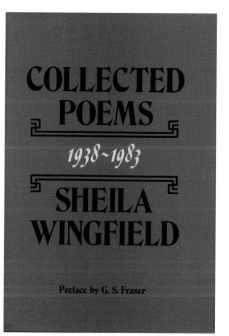

Miscellaneous volumes of *Collected Poems*

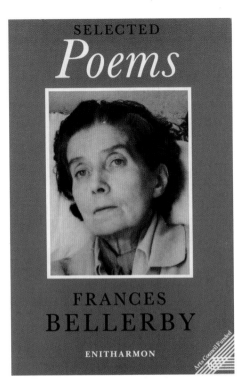

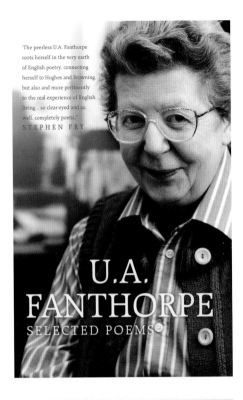

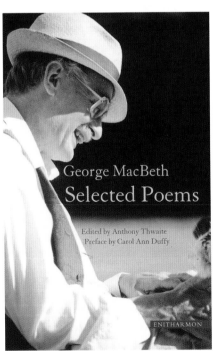

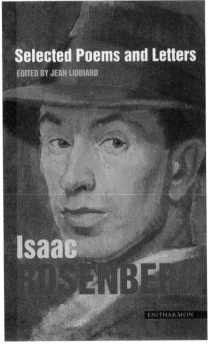

Miscellaneous volumes of *Selected Poems*

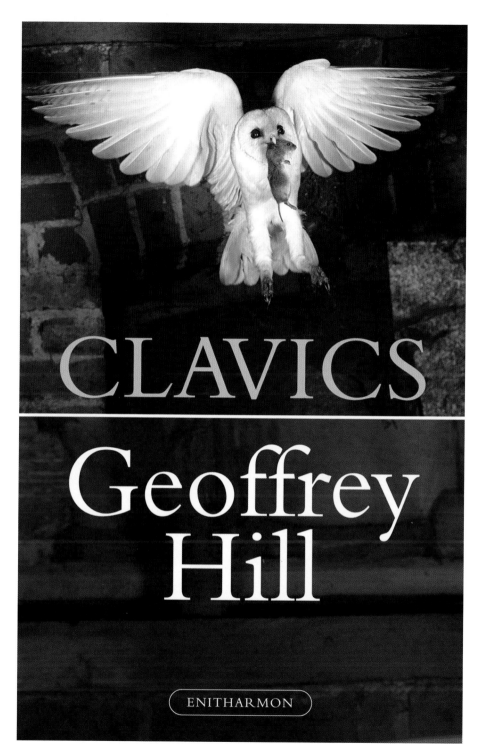

Dust-jacket of Geoffrey Hill's *Clavics* (2011)

RAINER MARIA
RILKE

Duino Elegies

ENITHARMON

Translated by Martyn Crucefix

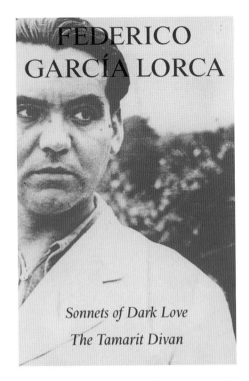

FEDERICO
GARCÍA LORCA

*Sonnets of Dark Love*

*The Tamarit Divan*

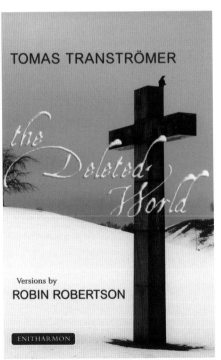

TOMAS TRANSTRÖMER

the Deleted World

Versions by
ROBIN ROBERTSON

ENITHARMON

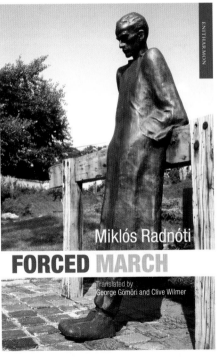

ENITHARMON

Miklós Radnóti

FORCED MARCH

Translated by
George Gömöri and Clive Wilmer

Front covers of selected translations

Front cover of Vladimir Mayakovsky's *Volodya* (2016)

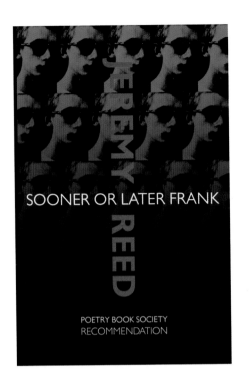

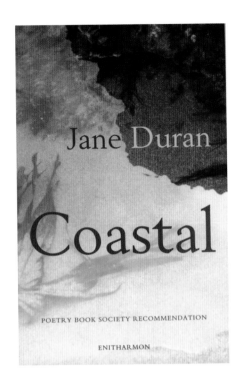

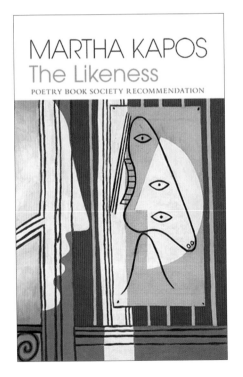

Poetry Book Society Recommendations

BILLY COLLINS

## Walking across the Atlantic

I wait for the holiday crowd to clear the beach
before stepping onto the first wave.

Soon I am walking across the Atlantic
thinking about Spain,
checking for whales, waterspouts.

I feel the water holding up my shifting weight.
Tonight I will sleep on its rocking surface.

But for now I try to imagine what
this must look like to the fish below,
the bottoms of my feet appearing, disappearing.


THE APPLE THAT ASTONISHED PARIS, 2006

RHIAN GALLAGHER

*The Wharf*


The shed side of town where rail lines converged
and a pointsman lowered and raised a wooden arm,
I breathed the oily air of passage, the sun
strobing off silos, and that indifference
that comes into my head at the moment
of departure, perhaps an inherited scent,
nosegays of immigration, the big lifting-up-of-your-life
borne to me on a chemical breeze, gun-metal
of a loading crane – cargoes. Those room-sized
corrugated containers, unmarked dry goods,
that blankness again, troubling
and longing like the place, loading
unloading – the very idea
of trading with the world.


I wasn't leaving. I was just walking under shadows
of the big ships that had stabled in the port,
water sluicing from their sides. I could hear them
ticking over, hear them strain on their ropes
their wider-than-my-arm ropes
skewered in knots as large as my head.
There was a sea-growth on everything: salt-scoured rusting,
barnacles on the tree-sides of the wharf, and those ropes,
with a catch of bladder weed and bull kelp.
The feeling of being not quite on land, the wharf
sleepers stained with the tar of old rail-lines,
keeping solid yet stationed in the drift.


SALT WATER CREEK, 2003

JOHN MONTAGUE

## *Speech Lesson*


I

The chant of those carriage wheels
As we chug towards Belfast;
Clickety-click, lickety-split,
*When will I learn again to speak?*


A straggle of villages before Dungannon:
Beragh, Carrickmore, Sixmilecross
(Forlorn stations, later bypassed)
Or *Will I never, ever speak again?*


II

*The Flower*
After hilly Dungannon, holy Donaghmore.
A cluster of convent girls clambers
Aboard the train, sweep and swirl
Past the place of the tongue-tied boy
Who huddles his head in his book
(which suddenly sheds all importance)
While they pile into the next compartment.
A chatter-and-clatter like starlings
As they settle. But one, bolder,
Tiptoes along the swaying corridor,
To risk a look where he sits, blushing.
Then another. A flurry of giggles.
Though as the troop leave, prodding one another,
The bold one turns, to throw him a flower.

III

Under the leather seats, the creak
Of iron wheels, as we steam towards Belfast:
*When will I learn again to speak?*
The Calvin Mills at Portadown,
Balmoral Show Grounds, and tethered
Above the wartime city, a silvery barrage balloon.
(Belfast's knell had not yet rung.)


IV

Near the bulky City Hall, 20 Wellington.
An ardent young Englishwoman,
Speaking of War and Poetry,
Places a hand on his tummy-tum-tum,
(The first stranger to have so done.)
'Young man, learn to speak from your diaphragm:
*Many merry men marched many times.*
And you should read Drummond Allison.
He was stationed here in Northern Ireland.'
She presses down, again and again:
'Consider our King: he broadcasts, stammering.
So let the wind whistle through your lungs.
And read poetry aloud, it can be such fun!
From how far away did you say you've come?'


V

Clickety-click, clickety-clack as
The Derry evening train ferries him back
All the way to County Tyrone and
Beragh Station, a lantern swaying
Along the platform. The parting whistle.
Then the long pull on his bicycle
Through the hay-scented countryside

To the turf-heavy hearth at home,
The  Rosary and a mug of Ovaltine
In the Sacred Heart-flushed kitchen.
Candle in hand, he climbs to his room.
A scurry of giggles, the shock of that flower.
*Many men marched many times:*
*Shall I begin to speak again?*

*I can still smell her perfume.*

LOVE POET, CARPENTER: MICHAEL LONGLEY AT SEVENTY,
*ed. Robin Robertson, 2009*

DOUGLAS DUNN

## Belfast to Edinburgh

At the beginning of descent, I see
Wind-turbines cast their giant, spinning arms.
The Southern Uplands send out false alarms,
Semaphore shadows, all waving to me.

Then, still descending, as the windows weep
Or something out beyond the tilted wing
Surrenders to the planet's suffering,
Plural phenomena that never sleep,

A far-off brightness shines on the wet plane.
A cockpit voice says something about doors.
The Forth Bridge is a queue of dinosaurs.

A field of poppies greets a shower of rain.

*LOVE POET, CARPENTER: MICHAEL LONGLEY AT SEVENTY,*
ed. Robin Robertson, 2009

NEIL CURRY

## St Kilda

I

The map the dominie had tacked up
On the schoolroom wall didn't even show
St Kilda, but then only a foreigner
Would have needed one to find his way past Mull
And Skye, out through the Sound of Harris, then on
For fifty empty miles over the
Oily pitch and swell of the grey
North Atlantic.
               Any St Kildans,
Out of sight of land, with bad weather closing,
Knew they'd only to watch the flight-paths
Of the birds: guillemot and gannet would wreck them
On the stacs round Borreray, while puffins
Scuttering back wave-high to Dun
Would prove a safe guide home to Hirta
And the Village Bay.


II

Birds. Or angels even
They must have seemed, the women
Plucking, in a cloud of feathers,
At the haul of fulmar their menfolk

Had themselves plucked off the cliffs
Of Conachair; cragsmen spidering,
Thirty fathoms down, along ledges
Of guano, dependent on sheer faith

In their neighbours and on a horsehair rope.
Claim life those cliffs could, but always would
Sustain it while there were sea-birds
In such thousands to stew or dry;

Even a gannet's neck, turned inside out,
Made a snug boot, and oil from the fulmar
Not only fuelled their lamps, but was a panacea
For no matter what ills or ailments of the island.


III

Ultima Thule it was
Until the Victorians discovered it,
Sending in their missionaries
To pound out the parable

Of the Prodigal Son
To people who hadn't
Anywhere to stray to
And had never seen a pig.

Then steamers came, and summer visitors
With gimcrack charities and new disease,
Tipping the cragsmen with a penny each
To see them capering about on Conachair;

Pennies that the winter ferryman
Would finger from the eyelids of their dead.

IV

By lantern-light
They loaded a few more
Sticks of furniture
And the last of the sheep,
And then they drowned their dogs.

In the morning,
According to custom,
In every empty house
There was a Bible left
Open at Exodus.

SHIPS IN BOTTLES, 1988

FRANCES BELLERBY

## The Exile

The fool said to the animals:
'You are merely my chattels,
With one lesson to learn –
That what happens to you is not your concern
But mine; for a just God has set
You on earth for my profit.'

The animals answered the fool
Nothing at all,
But for a single moment
Turned on him their wild, true, innocent
Eyes, where an Angel of the Lord
Holds Eden's flaming sword.

SELECTED POEMS, *ed. Anne Stevenson, 1986*

FRANCES HOROVITZ

*Irthing Valley*


a field of stones
a river of stones

each stone in its place

can a star be lost
or a stone?

uncountable
the constellations of stone

the wind lays itself down
                    at dusk
a fine cloth over the stones

the river is dispossessed
it casts up white branches
                    roots
shoals of white sand

it cannot oust its stones

between air and water
                    my shadow
laving the stones


COLLECTED POEMS, 1985 *in association*
*with Bloodaxe Books*

KEVIN CROSSLEY-HOLLAND

## An Approach to the Marsh

The rope is almost paid out here. Bawdeswell
and the ghost of its foul reeve left to stew,
I drive down cool green naves, and soon the lanes
begin to ripple. More pilgrims are shuffled off
to the shrine at Walsingham, and that is an end
to the firm ground of conviction. This is no man's land
that never belongs to earth or sea entirely:
now the flowing barley hemmed by screaming poppies,
a gull perched on a salt-rusted ploughshare
and a gull, a litter of blood-tarred feathers,
festering. A veil of butterflies, opalescent,
dips and quivers and rises, and I come to where
there is no going beyond.
                    Marsh, mud, shifting sand,
creeks sinuous and shining, they look sucked
and rendered almost certain by the sun;
but now and then, and for no evident reason,
rigging yaps, or seabirds shriek at what we cannot
even see, or the sea broadcasts over the marsh . . .
This bleached boat, that dabber, those children
gathering samphire, leaping over sun-crazed pulks:
the staithe today rests on its August oars;
hard light gives an edge to all that's apparent,
where nothing is what it seems or not for long.

SELECTED POEMS, 2001

148

TOMAS TRANSTRÖMER *versions by* ROBIN ROBERTSON

## Sketch in October

The tugboat is freckled with rust. What is it doing so far inland?
It's a heavy burnt-out lamp, tipped over in the cold.
But the trees still carry colours – wild signals to the other shore as if
someone wanted to be fetched home.

On the way back, I see mushrooms pushing up through the grass.
Stretching for help, these white fingers
belong to someone who sobs down there in the darkness.
We belong to the earth.

*THE DELETED WORLD, 2006*

JEREMY HOOKER

## At Salterns: A Memory of Mary Butts

1

No fossil world –

white walls,
domestic land
where furze grew wild,
and she – Blake's daughter – played.

White walls,
the days behind the day
blanked out, her passion
of possession gone.

But what is memory?

2

A fire that's autumn
in the light,
quick dartings in the trees,
a bird, a leaf, a word.

3

So much remains –
beech & conifer,
a glimpse of harbour water
and the distant Purbeck hills –
so much is changed.

But who can stop the passion
once released?

Each garden well an oracle.
Each tree the Tree of Life.


*SCATTERED LIGHT, 2015*

FRANCES HOROVITZ

# *Quanterness, Orkney 3,500 B.C.*


Not blood, but fact, from stones and the sieved dust.

'*Most die at twenty*'
                              – syllables snatched by wind.
Died of bone's ache, belly's ache,
                                        the ninth shining wave,
or long attrition of the absent sun.
'*Before the Pyramids, this death-house*
*was the centre of their lives*'.
Equal in death,
man, woman, young and old,
laid out for carrion, their wind-scoured bones
heaped hugger-mugger in the corbelled dark.
'*Some rodent bones were also found.*'

Each desperate spring
winds drift flower-scent from off the sea;
lambs call like children.
In warm heather
the young lie breast to breast
seeding the brief sun into their flesh.

Womb-hunger to outlast the stones.


WATER OVER STONE, 1980

JACK CLEMO

## On the Prospect of Leaving my Birthplace

Don't talk of my being uprooted
From the clay-beds of my childhood:
The man baptised, reborn, has no little father
Projecting him from a mould of infancy.
The boy could watch the white twisted fingers
Casting grim spells outside the cottage window
And be duly absorbed. I can't.

My roots are in my soul's Jerusalem,
Which has appeared in many forms
Of the warmed heart: Wimpole Street, Aldersgate Street,
Spurgeon's Tabernacle, Bernadette's shrine,
The Brownings' Florence and Barth's Safenwil.
How could the sick, fear-dazed child
At Goonamarris know of these?
Pit-blasts could not unearth the key
To my real self, the pilgrim-planted
Treasures of redemptive memory.

Clay-ravage was a fitting stage
For the doomed creature I seemed to my young mother,
Not for the happy husband I am to my wife,
Serene in mind and flesh, busily blending
Those foreign voices that broke the twisted clay-spell.

For nearly seventy years the slate roof
Has slanted above my sleep or my empty bed,
But the man I am, the fulfilled believer,
Needs palms, sweet modest hills and gentle

Cleansing ripples on the unhacked beach,
Not the rubble-wreckage of defiled meadows,
Or the iron teeth of an outgrown rejected cradle.

SELECTED POEMS, *ed. Luke Thompson, 2015*

PASCALE PETIT

*The Book of Trees*


I was in a floatplane, searching for a clear stretch
on the Javari river, then among the words.
Consonants towered above me blocking out the light.
I'd brought some gifts which I left on the riverbank
to lure a tribe never contacted by whites.
Soon I was following them into the Amazon.
We weaved through chapters tangled with lianas.

I could not speak to the Mayoruna
but their shaman planted thoughts in my head
which grew in my own language.
They were retreating to the beginning of time.
The girls were secluded for puberty rites.
The women burnt their belongings, their dead,
they could not take them back to their past.

The pages steepened.  Then we were above the treeline.
By day the pages had layers of dense sentences.
When night fell I could see nothing.  I had to feel my way
through this part of the book.  I learnt that one darkness
is rough, another smooth, yet another has thorns.
I learnt to read with all my nerve-endings.
I chewed manioc, sucked the venom from frogs' sacs.

I saw the twin waterfall at the source of the Javari
and the mountain which must not be viewed directly.
Morpho butterflies, with sky-blue wings and night-black
undersides, emerged from the cocoons of those words.
Then it rained harder than I have ever known rain,

forcing us downriver.  I was swept from the end of the story
back to the beginning.  I cannot get out of this book.

I have been changed by it as air is changed
when it passes through the pores of a leaf.

*HEART OF A DEER, 1998*

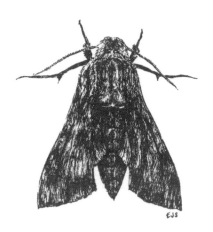

Erica Sail, *Moth*, drawing from Lawrence Sail's
*Songs of the Darkness* (2010)

HILARY DAVIES

*Covadonga*


Through tides of rain we drove the mountain road.
Rivers thrashed trees downstream beside us.
Far below, the ocean sucked and dug.

At Rio Seco the menfolk in the café
Signed themselves above the thick red waters.
Upon the road no-one among the mists and dripping beeches
No soul upon the road to Covadonga.

Covadonga! Water like thunder.
The little healing pool
Gone under God's surge.
The blast bulges outwards,
A new world birthing
All we fear may come,
And us beneath it.

Such little hopes,
Such sticks of momentariness
Caught in the ferns
An eyelash from the drop.
Everything we thought would hold us
Gives like cornerstones,
Like citadels, before the flood.
Onto this one thin ledge
We creep up under the overhang
To where our Lady of the Waterfalls
Keeps her courts of prayer.

Here is the all and only sanctuary
Our tiny bric-à-brac of suffering –
A piece of gauze, a notecard, a candle
Slung above the stupendous water.

Queen of our tragedy, bend your still face
Over the perpetual thunder; be with us when we go
Down over the anvil into the deep
And our soul's sounding.


EXILE AND THE KINGDOM, 2016

JOHN MOAT

## The Day of the Dead


Morning
beyond the mountains
the sun has begun to drum
light floods the lake

we came here to sleep
sleeping we began to dream
dreaming we began to dance
into the night

toward morning the dark wore thin
the spell grew less certain
then the dance led us back
under the arch of flowers

now beside the grave
the bread remains
chillies and wine
the pumpkin untouched

or so it appears
but before we departed
before sunrise in fact
the living had eaten.


*FIESTA & THE FOX REVIEWS HIS PROPHECY, 1980*

FRANCES CORNFORD

## Italian Siesta

Come from the glare to find
Your shuttered room most welcomingly blind
And white dimmed pillows on a waiting bed
That need your instant head.
This is no hour for sight,
Outside the colours are consumed by light;
The knitting women in the narrow street
Nod in the heat;
Flung down on his bleached nets
The fisherman forgets
Even the morning's catch he went to make
Where white rocks glisten under the hot lake.
Only the dry cicadas are awake
And scraping unremittingly repeat
A sound which is the very soul of heat.
There is no thought your dazzled mind can keep.
Come here and sleep.

SELECTED POEMS, *ed. Jane Dowson*, 1996

MYRA SCHNEIDER

## Thin White Girl

*after 'To a Fat Lady Seen from a Train' by Frances Cornford*


Oh why do you stride through the feathery grass,
hat pale as your hair and with back bared,
oh thin white girl, is it certainty of love
that makes you trample the park's green glory
now summer's unzipped?  Whatever your story
why not sit in the cool and coo like a dove?

The fat white woman – have you come across her
clumping through fields imprisoned in gloves –
the one tartly accused of missing so much?
Maybe she longed to be naked and touch
buttercup gold, whiskers soft as love,
ached to kiss seedheads and nuzzle clover.

And who are we to smirk and preen as we rush
about town in cages on wheels or slouch
in parks without spotting heron or spotted thrush?
And where is the insect that was crawling the beach
of my beige page?  It was red as my heart.
Oh why am I missing so much and so much?


*CIRCLING THE CORE, 2008*

DANNIE ABSE

## Sunbright

Sunbright sunbright, you said,
the first time we met in Venice
you, so alive with human light
I was dazzled black;
– like heavy morning curtains
in a sleeping bedroom
suddenly pulled back.

And the first time you undressed,
once more, I, frail-eyed,
undeservedly blessed,
as if it were a holy day,
as if it were yuletide,
and feeling a little drunk,
simply had to look away.

Well, circumspect Henry James
couldn't write *The Turn of the Screw*
till he turned his back on sunbright.
Chair around, just so,
to what was alive, beguiling,
in the Canaletto scene below.

Sweet, all this is true or virtually true.
It's only a poetry-licensed lie
when I rhyme and cheat and wink
and swear I almost need to wear
(muses help me, cross my heart) sunglasses
each time I think of you.

*IN EXTRA TIME, 2012*

HUBERT MOORE

## By the Rhône-Rhine Canal

Fingers entwining, maybe
an arm thrown over the shoulders,
these huge-limbed chestnut-trees
make all day every day evening
along our stretch of canal.

Here nothing is moving.  Water
brims in its water-trough; traffic
of time as of barges is obsolete.
All evening we sit, the two of us,
huge-limbed, weightless, by the canal,

as though, by opening sluices,
one or the other couldn't easily,
aimlessly drift down the map, through
widening gorges, to the river's mouth-
watering delta, les Bouches du Rhône,

or, merely locking off water,
float clean through Germany, further
and further northwards, high on the tide
of purer and purer Rhinewater,
up the sheer face of the map.

*ROLLING STOCK, 1991*

RUTGER KOPLAND *translated by* JAMES BROCKWAY

## No Reply

Give me the broad, the languid rivers,
the movements you do not see but sense,
the drinking willows, the aimless dykes,
a dead-still town along the shore.

Give me the winter, the wasted landscape,
the field bereft of a sign of life,
the resilience of the crackling heather.

Give me the cat as he looks before
he leaps, leaps to fight, leaps to flee,
to mate or to hunt.  As he looks.

Give me a horse in full gallop or
on his side in the grass.  Give me

a question, no reply.

*A WORLD BEYOND MYSELF, 1991*

CAROL RUMENS

*Before these Wars*


In the early days of marriage
my parents go swimming in an empty sea,
cold as an echo, but somehow *theirs,*
for all its restless size.

From the year 1980 I watch them
putting on the foamy lace.
The sun's gold oils slide from their young skin
and hair, as they surface

to fling each other handfuls
of confetti – iced tinsel
and tissue, miniature horseshoes
of silver, white poppy petals.

I search their laughter in vain:
no baby twinkles there,
no Hitler marches on Poland
through the cornflower waves

this print shows pewter.
But that the impossible happens
eventually, everyone knows.
And when they swim away

the unsettled water fills
with shuddery, dismantled weddings,
a cloud unfurled like an oak-tree,
time twisting as it burns.

PARENTS: AN ANTHOLOGY OF POEMS BY WOMEN WRITERS,
ed. Myra Schneider and Dilys Wood, 2000

GRETA STODDART

## A Hundred Sheep in a Green Field

The way our mother said something
under her breath made us suddenly hush
in the back and not ask why we'd slowed
to barely a crawl or why we were told
to roll up the windows and sit tight
and *Everything is going to be all right.*
Our faces, soon waxy with sweat,
mooned out against the glass as we crept
alongside cars where men, alone
in suits, breathed in and out their own
serene and air-conditioned air.

Slowly, we came upon the scene:
under a big, blue sky
the lovely smell of petrol rose
in seething ribbons,
and a woman in a torn summer dress
was dragging her body across the lanes
where bits of toy, car, family
lay like the remains of a picnic,
and a man's head lay sleeping on the wheel.

Then I saw beyond this
to a hundred sheep in a green field
eating their cheerless way through the earth;
eating, eating, until in time,
I thought, they'll reach the red hot centre
and find themselves falling,
stiff and stupid as tables,
into that burning pit.

The rain started when we crossed the border
and didn't stop once the whole summer.
We had to light fires in every room;
even the sheets smelled of coal.
My sister sat at the window
closing and opening the curtain
onto an empty, shining field.

TYING THE SONG, *ed. Mimi Khalvati and Pascale Petit, 2000*

HILARY DAVIES

## Beachy Head

I see you now, my mother and father,
Coming up this cliff slowly, though you did
So but yesterday, as if you are long dead.
Here my father, placing his legs askew
As he pulls for breath, turns to look back
Down the twisting path they have come.
My mother touches her arthritic knee.
And all around, the great arc of the world
Encloses them.  O keep back from the dazzling edge,
Daddy, don't move with your vertigo closer
To the drop, the terrible slippage.
Lay out your provisions and go giddy
With the clouds running overhead.
And my mother unwraps the boiled eggs,
Lets tea from the thermos, lies down close
To the ticking grass while across to France
The years flash back and forth
With their insistent whisper, hish, hish,
Lullaby, wash away our hurt down the shingle;
How these two rheumaticky people shimmer
Like gods in the grass.

*THE SHANGHAI OWNER OF THE BONSAI SHOP, 1991*

## ELIZABETH GARRETT

## *Vista*

Standing, with your back turned, taut at work,
Wearing the day's frosted willow-grey skirt
Like a bell of smoke, while a child went on colouring
Under the spell of the Lakeland-Cumberland arc,
You turned suddenly hearing the doorbell ring.
Turned? No – *spun*, till the skirt flared its carillon
And all the poplar leaves of the world shone
Silver, their green gone in the wind's turning.

And here I am, wise at the open door
Trying to remember what it was I came for,
Struck by a knowledge of beauty years beyond
Anything I had yet come to understand,
Watching you disappear down that corridor
Of brilliant sound, my stolen breath in your hand.

BRANCH-LINES: EDWARD THOMAS AND CONTEMPORARY
POETRY, ed. Guy Cuthbertson and Lucy Newlyn, 2007

PETER SCUPHAM

*The Map-Maker*


The sound of the paper – surely that's the same?
Open it out.  Sprung on my finger ends
the resistance is purposive, a clean flip.
On the obverse, four spots of glue hold nothing, tightly,
their ochres caked and crystalline.  He spreads it out
as I spread it now, smoothing its awkward lie.
Folds guide small rivulets of shade, flats cream
under gaslight, or whiten in the profligate sun.

This is how he sees it.  Rather, how what he sees
in the beck, the lane, the heat-haze over the wolds
can be dried and certified, held like the moths
in his killing-bottle.  Catlike, he marks his journeys.
Ink runs thinly, darkens.  He sows words broadcast,
dips the scratch-pen, straight-edges the railway,
as outside, hot verges coarsen with umbellifers:
*Lineside.  Tiger beetles, flowers, Lepidoptera in general.*

His head adrift with flutterings, sheen and texture,
he pushes his way through millions of green and brown,
holding tight to a spinning signpost of names.
His tracks race off the paper through *Nova Scotia,*
*J. Scupham, July 9, 1916.*  In brightest Lincolnshire
my twelve-year-old father carefully encodes
*Hill, Clearing, Viper's Bugloss, Yellow Underwings,*
ransacks *America* for its *Heaths and Tigers* –

the large Heath (*Epinephele Tithonus*),
the Scarlet Tiger (*Callimorpha Dominula*) –
this Midsummer, his 'Prize for Nature Study'
is Furneaux' *British Butterflies and Moths*.
With bruised laurel, cyanide of potassium,
the countryside may be coaxed into your trap
and, later, secured by silver, black or gilded pins.
Be sure the poison does not merely stupefy,

leaving you horrified, when your box is opened,
'by the sight of the poor victim struggling to free itself',
a teeming landscape unwilling to lie down.
I refold his paper, packed with nests and burrows,
thickets of skin and fur. Ink and copy-pencil
shine briefly against my lamp, keep the dry glaze
lost by close on a hundred years of eyes.
The dead rustle back to nest with a stir of wings;

the annular rings thicken and simplify.
I could stand there still, lost in a no-man's-land,
holding his childhood's trench-map, think of his brother
laying his gun-sights somewhere on the Somme,
consider how folds of dead ground foster rivulets,
hedges whiten to blackthorn, cream to hawthorn.
As he dies, I ask how he spends the time,
bedbound. 'Oh, just go for walks,' he answers.

BRANCH-LINES: EDWARD THOMAS AND CONTEMPORARY
POETRY, ed. Guy Cuthbertson and Lucy Newlyn, 2007

## MIMI KHALVATI

## *Coma*

*Mr Khalvati?* Larger than life he was;
too large to die so they wired him up on a bed.
Small as a soul he is on the mountain ledge.

Lids gone thin as a babe's. If it's mist he sees
it's no mist he knows by name. *Can you hear me,
Mr Khalvati?* Larger than life he was

and the death he dies large as the hands that once
drowned mine and the salt of his laugh in the wave.
Small as a soul he is on the mountain ledge.

*Can you squeeze my hand?* (Ach! Where are the hands
I held in mine to pull me back to the baize?)
*Mr Khalvati?* Larger than life he was

with these outstretched hands that squeezing squeeze
thin air. Wired he is, tired he is and there,
small as a soul he is on the mountain ledge.

No nudging him out of the nest. No one to help him
fall or fly, there's no coming back to the baize.
*Mr Khalvati?* Larger than life he was.
Small as a soul he is on the mountain ledge.

PARENTS: AN ANTHOLOGY OF POEMS BY WOMEN
WRITERS, ed. *Myra Schneider and Dilys Wood, 2000*

MYRA SCHNEIDER

*Leave Taking*


And when he was struck speechless
then I wanted him to speak again,
when he couldn't deliver the orders
I wanted to cram back into his mouth,
break the unbearable waters
of wrath over my head
then I wanted to hear his voice again,
would have held out cupped hands
for a command, a judgement, a complaint.

When he was sentenced
to a wordless struggle for breath
and could no longer devour us
with: *I'm dying . . . I wish I was dead,*
I discovered what I'd guessed:
he'd cried wolf instead of pain,
stalked by implacable terrors
he dared not name. But he'd given
doctors instructions to haul him
back for the last mile, last inch

to keep tabs on the world,
its disgraceful conduct of itself,
his daughters' failings, successes
and the complex finances in his head.
Minutes before his lungs
finally rebelled
his fingers plotted in the air
the upward curve of a grandson's career.

And in those four days
when his eyes fixed
on the precise saline drip
drip through glass arteries,
when his hands washed themselves
of the universe or clutching at a pen
produced strange new writing,
did a kind of acceptance trickle through?

In those four speechless days
I began to strip him of shortcomings,
bury the terrible damages
and I hung onto his zest,
his generosities, his ever-
enquiring scientific mind,
his hunger for consciousness,
that miracle each person carries,
a delicate globe lit
by intricate, unseen filaments
which is so suddenly put out,
which is totally
irreplaceable.

INSISTING ON YELLOW: NEW AND SELECTED
POEMS, 2000

EDWIN BROCK

## *On the First Stroke*

Someone had murdered someone
somewhere again.  It was a black space
running away from fear
and I did not know how much to give it.

It was not dying but death
of love.  And not one love
but everything.  It was like trying
to go straight through
from one fear to another
without love.
It was abandonment.

Someone was singing Do not forsake me
O my darling.  It is for later.
When I remember.  When the wind
that blows me from the beginning dies down.

It is always becoming dark
and I am worried that the ladies
allow me to walk from one night to another
with no-one to look after me.
I am afraid and pull the black blanket up
to just below my eyes and look over it.

There is a cliff road from Cromer
that flows between sand and shingle
and the cold North Sea
carrying us in black spaces of fear
above hotels and hospitals
piers and sharp white lights.

I am remembering:
it is the same voice singing
Do not forsake me O my darling
and the crying has begun.


*AND ANOTHER THING*, 1999

PASCALE PETIT

## The Burning

Bury me up to my neck
in the sands of my father's desert.

Down in the Great Emptiness
let the fire of his country

burn my face all day.
If I lose consciousness

revive me
only at night

with a sip of water from the Styx
and a sip from the Acheron,

bring me samples of all rivers
from the Old World and the New.

When my father finally appears,
moisten my mouth with a drop

from the Phlegethon – river of flames,
my thirst

will teach me the words
to draw him to me.

I'll breathe very deeply,
sucking the brown dust that is his flesh

into every inch of my lungs,
until there is no more of his power left on the earth.

Only then may you seal my lips with a thorn
to keep my soul-force in.


*HEART OF A DEER, 1998*

PHOEBE HESKETH

## Second Childhood

Free as a thistle, white hair blowing,
he wanders through fields
leaving gates open as he leaves doors at home.
Without direction his days are slanted
by shadow and sun
easy as a weathercock swinging
on the wind's heel.
Pulling sorrel seeds through finger and thumb
he scatters the coral beads,
tramples buttercups to gold-dust on his boots.

High time is harvest; a bronze moon
hangs over the hill;
by day the sun
ripens slowly as red fruit.
Wading through sand-coloured corn,
he snatches the prawn-whiskered barley
to play with all winter.

*Cuckoo! Cuckoo!* Grass-blade to mouth
he answers the bodiless voice,
wonder-gazing into the wide blue
bowl of infinity.

Happy, happy – this childhood is surer
than a child's,
unthreatened, outlasting life.

*THE LEAVE TRAIN: NEW AND SELECTED POEMS, 1994*

STEPHEN WATTS

## from *My Mother, Her Tongue*

When your ashes were scattered you became
      those flowers, you became
these trees, you became those birds that fling
their songs across torn webs of sky leaping
      from goblets of light

You are not ashes, you are a tree unfurled
      from where the soil and air
are slung against a silent wind that folds me
back from despair, o language coming from
      you white as jasmine

You've flown between the frost and the sun,
      you never were ash
in the charnel-house, the ordinary guards of
death had no meaning before the jasmine
      of your face

Now your body is gone and your discourse,
      your spirit like a bird is flown,
I strain to measure your voice in my lungs
but I know colliding rivers have loosed
      my mother tongue

I was not there when the bird of your soul
      flew off from your body, I
could not watch that final trance and when
I was late come your breath was no longer
      making

Its slow unmeasured dance across the floor,
    when I got to your death your
mouth was already set in its trancing curve,
your nose was held and bent against those
        jasmines of your face


*ANCIENT SUNLIGHT, 2014*

ELIZABETH JENNINGS

## One Flesh

Lying apart now, each in a separate bed,
He with a book, keeping the light on late,
She like a girl dreaming of childhood,
All men elsewhere – it is as if they wait
Some new event: the book he holds unread,
Her eyes fixed on the shadows overhead.

Tossed up like flotsam from a former passion,
How cool they lie.  They hardly ever touch,
Or if they do it is like a confession
Of having little feeling – or too much.
Chastity faces them, a destination
For which their whole lives were a preparation.

Strangely apart, yet strangely close together,
Silence between them like a thread to hold
And not wind in.  And time itself's a feather
Touching them gently.  Do they know they're old,
These two who are my father and my mother
Whose fire from which I came has now grown cold?

PARENTS: AN ANTHOLOGY OF POEMS BY WOMEN
WRITERS, ed. Myra Schneider and Dilys Wood, 2000

MARTYN CRUCEFIX

## Tiger

I had a tiger suck my fist last night.
A warm, wet clasp that owed everything

to the child who yesterday held my thumb.
Sleep changed her to this striped killer

though I felt no fear, nor could I see
why the world was not as I'd been told.

Its canines were yellowed, big as my thumb.
My hand glistened, saliva-wrinkled.

I saw the cat plead just as it was shot –
its crew-cut pelt punctured five times

each blast received like an electric shock,
growing less and less . . .

Spreadeagled across the bonnet of a jeep
at the mud village, a thousand file past

to touch a paw, stroke a hollowed ear.
The cat, last night, hung so leaden-heavy

on my hand as did the child yesterday,
a warm, wet mouth wanting everything.

*AN ENGLISH NAZARETH, 2004*

ANNA ADAMS

## Scarp Song

My two strong sons skate out in one small shoe
        treading the polished water
across inverted hills that hang stone heads
among the white clouds in its green glass mirror.

The wind sleeps, and a blanket mist may thicken,
        hiding the polished water,
and no one knows which breathing wind may cloud
the glass, and frost or shiver the green mirror.

All my love's work sits in that far white boat,
        trusting the smiling traitor,
diminishes beyond duststorms of birds.
I see long threads of white hair in the mirror.

My sons ride fearlessly, far out to sea;
        I would not have them other:
they cheat the traitor of his mackerel shoal
and teach the lobster to repent his error.

Northeaster, chase them home; bring rainbow weather
        across the ruffled water.
Confine, Southwest, remorseless water-walls
that travel blind.  I dare not name my terror.

GREEN RESISTANCE: NEW AND SELECTED POEMS, 1996

JANE DURAN

## Forty-Eight

Once a month I expect that I am pregnant.
My body takes that liberty –
in the street I am full of misgivings, armfuls,
my breasts manage the joy of being painful.

I expect that the gleaning has taken hold,
the warrior gates have closed
and the town turned heavy inside
with its gold, its tarnish of silver.
I expect the little known
to be drumming and corded,
my belly to be amazed and striated
with new boundaries.

There will be no going back,
once a month.
Nowhere will the bereft be local.
They will not be in their usual cafés.
They will be overlooking seaports
and their voices will drop with evening
so as not to wake the children.
No one will be childless
nor the haze hide a bay.

There are slip landings in my belly,
the tug of the mollusc love,
its impersonal kiss unfolded
its wish-kiss lying low
left behind when the sea goes out and stops
for my foot to go oops on the slippery rock.

When the blood lies out on its shoal,
when the blood arrives
on the sloop, on the stoop, like a sailor,
like an acrobat, like electricity,
I will say it is not really that.
No, no.  I am not ready.


BREATHE NOW, BREATHE, 1995

Gwen Raverat, *Mother and Child*, block cut of 1934
from Frances Cornford's *Selected Poems* (1996)

PHOEBE HESKETH

## I Give Death to a Son

Rhythmic pincer-jaws clench
and widen – the world explodes –
I give death to a son.
Tearing apart the veil he comes
protected fish from dark pool.
I push him over the weir,
land him on dry stones.

Was he anything, anywhere
behind, beyond,
out there in nothingness?
Is he nothing, made aware
of cold, hunger, nakedness?

Trailing glory and slime
he is washed and dried,
grave-clothes ready warmed
by the fireside.

THE LEAVE TRAIN: NEW AND SELECTED
POEMS, 1994

FRANCES HOROVITZ

## In Painswick Churchyard

'Is this where people are buried?
I will not let them bury you'

He picnics among tombs
– pours imaginary tea,
a yew tree his kitchen

'You will live with me in my house'

Oh could I believe the living and the dead inhabit one house
under the sky
and you my child run into your future for ever

WATER OVER STONE, 1980

GEORGE MacBETH

## The Red Herring
*after Cros*


There was once a high wall, a bare wall. And
against this wall, there was a ladder,
a long ladder.  And on the ground,
under the ladder, there was a red
herring.  A dry red herring.

And then a man came along. And in his hands
(they were dirty hands) this man had
a heavy hammer, a long nail
(it was also a sharp nail) and
a ball of string.  A thick ball of string.

All right.  So the man climbed up
the ladder (right up to the top)
and knocked in the sharp nail:
spluk! Just like that.
Right on top of the wall. The bare wall.

Then he dropped the hammer. It dropped
right down to the ground. And onto the nail
he tied a piece of string, a long
piece of string, and onto the string
he tied the red herring. The dry red herring.

And let it drop. And then he climbed
down the ladder (right down
to the bottom), picked up the hammer
and also the ladder (which was pretty heavy)
and went off. A long way off.

And since then, that red herring, the dry
red herring on the end of the string, which is
quite a long piece, has been
very very slowly swinging and
swinging to a stop. A full stop.

I expect you wonder why I made
up this story, such a simple story. Well,
I did it just to annoy people.
Serious people. And perhaps also
to amuse children. Small children.

SELECTED POEMS, *ed. Anthony Thwaite, 2002*

## LEE HARWOOD

### *Childish*

From the top balcony of a pagoda
in the Royal Botanic Gardens
you step
            out into the air,
step from treetop to treetop
then swoop through the air to further trees
– as a bird, though not – and
on bright spring days shoot up to
those glittering white clouds and
walk the skies.

These day dreams that carry you through.

And to the south,
late one evening on a balcony by the sea,
a note flutters down        written by a child.
It says 'Do not disturb the angel'.

Words like that shower of sparks
as welders hunch over their job
cutting and joining beams.

So much hope in such moments
wherever they may happen
without reason or purpose, but there.

The gardens spread off into a green haze of trees,
woods that may border a river or a busy city road.
A calm as you gaze into an unknown distance.

Late at night standing, watching.
The sound of the waves breaking on the shore,
the lights of passing freighters out to sea.

The next morning the red handrail of the pagoda
glistens with raindrops.


*THE ORCHID BOAT, 2014*

SIMON RAE

## That Single Thread

His plan was to do exactly what he did.
All his actions hung from that single thread.
You could call him wilful but he wasn't stupid.

He knew what he was up for and he vid-
eo'd it as he did it in his head.
His plan was to do exactly what he did.

He was the archivist from whom nothing was hid
with regard to the far corner under his brother's bed.
You could call him wayward but he wasn't stupid.

To meet him he was just like any kid.
Life had taught him all the things he needed.
His plan was to do exactly what he did.

He wanted to know what bubbled under the lid,
what the odds were and whether the truth bled.
You could call him wanton but he wasn't stupid.

He didn't need to be all that intrepid.
*Don't even think about screaming* was what he said.
His plan was to do exactly what he did.
You could call him evil but he wasn't stupid.

*GIFT HORSES, 2006*

ROGER MOULSON

## The Riding Room

Bare boards, curtains of dust all stuck together
and the horse's tail glued in its bottom. The hairs
aren't dead for when we yank at them half-scared
the horse leaps in the air and breaks its tether,
and then kicks back. Dust rises from the rockers
between boards stained like gravy round the skirting.
Smack smack its round grey side. It doesn't hurt it.
Giddyup. Beneath the window is the knocker.

Mysterious callers come to our front door
and there's a Wolseley with an oval light.
Rock gently. Shsh. We rock across the floor
over the heads of Mr and Mrs Brown
who shout and scream when we're awake at night.
Rock rock we both go up we both come down.

WAITING FOR THE NIGHT-ROWERS, 2006

C. DAY LEWIS

## Walking Away
*for Sean*


It is eighteen years ago, almost to the day –
A sunny day with the leaves just turning,
The touch-lines new-ruled – since I watched you play
Your first game of football, then, like a satellite
Wrenched from its orbit, go drifting away

Behind a scatter of boys. I can see
You walking away from me towards the school
With the pathos of a half-fledged thing set free
Into a wilderness, the gait of one
Who finds no path where the path should be.

That hesitant figure, eddying away
Like a winged seed loosened from its parent stem,
Has something I never quite grasp to convey
About nature's give-and-take – the small, the scorching
Ordeals which fire one's irresolute clay.

I have had worse partings, but none that so
Gnaws at my mind still. Perhaps it is roughly
Saying what God alone could perfectly show –
How selfhood begins with a walking away,
And love is proved in the letting go.


SELECTED POEMS, *ed. Jill Balcon, 2004*

MARTHA KAPOS

*Eye*


I looked for your eye.  I looked
for any light at all staring

from the body's long house at night
where it lay stretched out

full length between trees, its grey roof shut
its impenetrable dark back turned

and I imagined from the other side
I'd see your very wide lit face

its innumerable yellow rooms

two children playing
their light heads together laughing.


*THE LIKENESS, 2014*

SIMON ARMITAGE

from *Out of the Blue*\*


4

Arranged on the desk
among rubber bands and bulldog clips:

here is a rock from Brighton beach,
here is a beer-mat, here is the leaf

of an oak, pressed and dried, papery thin.
Here is a Liquorice Allsorts tin.

A map of the Underground pinned to the wall.
The flag of St George.  A cricket ball.

Here is a calendar, counting the days.
Here is a photograph snug in its frame:

this is my wife on our wedding day,
here is a twist of her English hair.

Here is a picture in purple paint:
two powder-paint towers, heading for space,

plus rockets and stars and the Milky Way,
plus helicopters and aeroplanes.

*Jelly-copters and fairy-planes.*
In a spidery hand, underneath it, it says,

'If I stand on my toes can you see me wave?'

5

The towers at one.
The silent prongs of a tuning fork,
testing the calm.

Then a shudder or bump.
A juddering thump or a thud.
I swear no more

than a thump or a thud.
But a Pepsi Max jumps out of its cup.
And a filing cabinet spews its lunch.

And the water-cooler staggers then slumps.
Then a sonic boom and the screen goes blue.
Then a deep, ungodly dragon's roar.

Then ceiling tiles, all awry at once,
and a soft, white dust snowing down from above.
See, there in the roof,

the cables, wires, pipes and ducts,
the veins and fibres and nerves and guts,
exposed and unstrung.

In their shafts, the lift-cars clang
and the cables are plucked:
a deep, sub-human, inaudible twang.

And a lurch.
A pitch.
A sway to the south.

I know for a fact these towers can stand
the shoulder-charge of a gale force wind
or the body-check of hurricane.

But this is a punch, a hammer-blow.
I sense it thundering underfoot,
a pulsing, burrowing, aftershock,

down through the bone-work of girders and struts,
down into earth and rock.
Right to the root.

The horizon totters and lists.
The line of the land seems to teeter
on pins and stilts,

a perceptible tilt.
Then the world re-aligns, corrects itself.
Then hell lets loose.

And I know we are torn.
I know we are holed
because through that hole

a torrent of letters and memos and forms
now streams and storms
now flocks and shoals
now passes and pours
now tacks and jibes
now flashes and flares
now rushes and rides
now flaps and glides . . .

the centrefold of the *New York Times*
goes winging by

then a lamp
a coat
a screen
a chair

a yoghurt pot
a yucca plant
a yellow cup
a Yankees cap.

A shoe, freeze-framed against the open sky.
I see raining flames.
I see hardware fly.


OUT OF THE BLUE, 2008

Hughie O'Donoghue, *Head of Cresseid*, etching from the *de luxe* edition of
Seamus Heaney's *The Testament of Cresseid* (2004)

Paula Rego, *Flood*, etching reproduced in Blake Morrison's *Pendle Witches* (1996)

Jim Dine, *Paintbrush*, lithograph accompanying Robert Creeley's
poems in *Pictures* (2001)

Tony Bevan, *Open Corridor*, tipped-in image from Harold Pinter's
*The Disappeared and other poems* (2002)

Christopher Le Brun, *Atalanta and Hippomenes*, etching from the *de luxe* edition of
Ted Hughes's *Shakespeare's Ovid* (1995)

Peter Blake, *Circus Acts*, collage from *Paris Escapades* (2011)

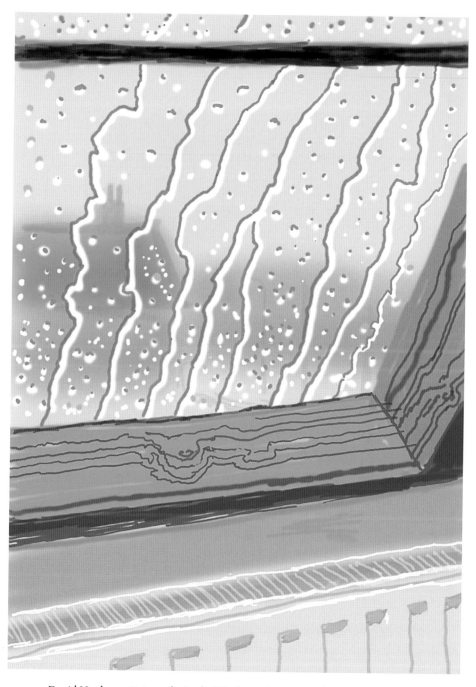

David Hockney, *Rain on the Studio Window*, inkjet-printed computer drawing
from the *de luxe* edition of *My Yorkshire* (2011)

Duane Michals, photogravure etching from the *de luxe* edition of
*The House I Once Called Home* (2003)

JOHN KINSELLA

## Painted Bellows
*after Alfred Wallis*


The dead lung breathes
without a will of its own;
a trick of forgotten thought,
a knee-jerk reaction.  By the dark
fireplace – before first light chills
panes and water, the necromancy
of seas and tide, harbour and boat –
the pursed lips blow hard
into embers: a false sun
throws light just as the tide
bluffs recovery.  In our mind's eye,
our breath frozen on the window,
we blow up a storm.


MARINE, 2015

DANNIE ABSE

## Blue Song*

Some things there always are,
some things a man must lose,
Picasso paints a guitar,
that way he sings the Blues.

Russian cows jump over the moon
(very strong is Russian booze)
but Chagall's cow never lands,
otherwise he'd sing the Blues.

Rothko squares a mirror with blood
(there's blood in his every bruise).
Paints his own reflection out
and soundlessly sings the Blues.

Moon-faced Francis Bacon
eerily shrieks and spews
humanoid freaks into a cage.
Odd way to sing the Blues.

Body detective Lucian Freud
magnifies his sexless nudes
– the uglier the better.
That's how he sings the Blues.

The aloneness of the artist!
D. Hockney paints his trees in twos
and Time, itself, in colours passing
– a covert way to sing the Blues.

Damian likes his sheep well pickled,
I prefer my meat in stews.
Let collectors shed their millions.
Soon they'll sing the Blues.

Do I wish to be a painter
acclaimed with buffs' reviews?
All I lack is talent.
That's why I sing the Blues.

*IN EXTRA TIME, 2012*

JEREMY REED

## Stormy Weather

Take me so bluely, greyly, stormily,
and always blackly, inconclusively,
into that bluesy, jazzy song,
it's Lena Horne, or Billie Holiday,
perhaps even Sinatra's rounding out
of love's moody, sad inequalities
I'm playing on this rainy day,

reflecting on old unrequited love
left like a red glove on the beach
for the highest wave to retrieve
and scoop into the frothy swash.
Don't easy couples marry on the beach? –

a black car standing by for a white dress
a black dress standing by for a white car.
Billie could find no equal in a man.

Pre-thunder clarity, and sassy pinks
luminous under density
building as massive cumulus.
Something will break; a sonic riff

bring back the sharpest memories,
the ones that bite like lemon juice.
I play it over, 'Stormy Weather',
the way she gets the rhyme on 'together',
before the vampish hurt breaks through
gritty with memories, and the fast rain
orchestrates every shade of moody blue.

SAINT BILLIE, 2001

U.A. FANTHORPE

## Patience Strong

Everyone knows her name.  Trite calendars
Of rose-nooked cottages or winding ways
Display her sentiments in homespun verse
Disguised as prose.  She has her tiny niche
In women's magazines, too, tucked away
Among the recipes or near the end
Of some perennial serial.  Her theme
Always the same: rain falls in every life,
But rainbows, bluebirds, spring, babies or God
Lift up our hearts.  No doubt such rubbish sells.
She must be feathering her inglenook.
Genuine poets seldom coin the stuff,
Nor do they flaunt such aptly bogus names.
Their message is oblique; it doesn't fit
A pocket diary's page; nor does it pay.

One day in epileptic outpatients,
A working-man, a fellow in his fifties,
Was feeling bad.  I brought a cup of tea.
He talked about his family and job:
His dad was in the Ambulance Brigade;
He hoped to join, but being epileptic,
They wouldn't have him.  *Naturally*, he said,
*With my disease, I'd be a handicap.*
*But I'd have liked to help.*  He sucked his tea,
Then from some special inner pocket brought
A booklet muffled up in cellophane,
Unwrapped it gently, opened at a page –
Characteristic cottage garden, seen

Through chintzy casement windows.  Underneath
Some cosy musing in the usual vein,
And *See*, he said, *this is what keeps me going.*


*BEROWNE'S BOOK*, 2015

DAVID GASCOYNE

## Apologia

'Poète et non honnête homme.'
                    Pascal

1

It's not the Age,
Disease, or accident, but sheer
Perversity (or so one must suppose),
That pins me to the singularly bare
Boards of this trestle-stage
That I have mounted to adopt the pose
Of a demented wrestler, with gorge full
Of phlegm, eyes bleared with salt, and knees
Knocking like ninepins: a most furious fool!

2

Fixed by the nib
Of an inept pen to a bleak page
Before the glassy stare of a ghost mob,
I stand once more to face the silent rage
Of my unseen Opponent, and begin
The same old struggle for the doubtful prize:
Each stanza is a round, and every line
A blow aimed at the too elusive chin
Of that Oblivion which cannot fail to win.

3

Before I fall
Down silent finally, I want to make
One last attempt at utterance, and tell
How my absurd desire was to compose
A single poem with my mental eyes
Wide open, and without even one lapse
From that most scrupulous Truth which I pursue
When not pursuing Poetry. – Perhaps
Only the poem I can never write is *true*.


SELECTED POEMS, 1994

GEOFFREY HILL

from *Clavics*

8

How far give attestation its free ride –
A fair question.  Poetry is eccentric
       Labour of pride;
       Fixates power;
       Fixes mantric
       Pitch and con trick;
     Nor hewer nor drawer;
      Not romantic.
Claim that it rises to its own jerked bait
Cites polity its *raison* among such
       Affairs of State
       You, I, might name,
       Set within touch
       Of heightened speech
    In  s o m e  a w e d  i n t e r i m.
       *You believe that?*
I remit your citations, Lord Apollo,
Bestower of conundrums.  Try me: what
       Flex to allow
Fixing this swing-arm with its counterweight.

•

Listen to and make music while you can
　Pray *Mater ora Filium*
　　Cry *Spem in Alium*
　　God is made man
　　　Choric
　　　Ly r i c
　　Heaven receives
　Impartial these tributes
Creation call it that believes
Even to blasphemy in our ranged throats.


　　　　9


Edgy, you say, cagy, strange edginess.
Check the electric circuits, you booby.
　　　Brushes a mess;
　　　Check them again;
　　　A fine hobby!
　　　Feeling clubby
　　Largely eases the pain.
　　　Perish nobly.
Should benefit from this mixed blood and flame
Utterance known first to the haruspex
　　　And then to fame.
　　　Best are logged on
　　　By paradox
　　　As with drab sex
　　By desire to have done
　　　Old meretrix.
Mystic emendation shall be called for;
Metaphysical  intensifiers
　　　Well enrolled-for.
Not all the bad poets are bad liars.


　　　　•


218

Revealed thus as a type of figured bass
　　Enriched ad libitum by hand
　　　Of cute accompanist:
　　　　Hear the quills click
　　　　　*My son*
　　　　　*My son*
　　　　The strings are slack
　　　Will Lawes is *broke* at Chest-
　　Er; Lycidas lies in the sand;
Both justified.　England rides rich on loss.


*CLAVICS, 2011*

ANTHONY THWAITE

## Essays in Criticism

I like this more than that.
That is better than this.
This means this and that.
That is what this one wrote.
This is not that at all.
This is no good at all.
Some prefer this to that
But frankly this is old hat.
This is what Thissites call
Inferior this, and yet
I hope I have shown you all
That that way lies a brick wall
Where even to say 'Yes, but . . .'
Confuses the this with the that.

Instead, we must ask 'What is this?'
Then, 'Is that *that* sort of this,
Or a modified this, or a miss
As good as a mile, or a style
Adopted by that for this
To demonstrate thisness to those
Who expect a that-inclined prose
Always from this one – a stock
Response from readers like these.'
But of course the whole thing's a trick
To make you place *them* among those
Who only follow their nose,
Who are caught on the this/that spike
But who think they know what they like.

SELECTED POEMS 1956–1996, 1997

EDWARD DORN

*The Surrealist*


rode roaring
clutched the handles
                    spread wide
                    from the shoulders,

his black motorcycle flinching.
And behind him bounced
doggedly the trailer bearing
higher, a like cycle,
Black.


*DERELICT AIR: FROM COLLECTED OUT, 2015*

DAVID GASCOYNE

## The Very Image
*To René Magritte*


An image of my grandmother
her head appearing upside-down upon a cloud
the cloud transfixed on the steeple
of a deserted railway station
far away

An image of an aqueduct
with a dead crow hanging from the first arch
a modern-style chair from the second
a fir tree lodged in the third
and the whole scene sprinkled with snow

An image of the piano tuner
with a basket of prawns on his shoulder
and a firescreen under his arm
his moustache made of clay-clotted twigs
and his cheeks daubed with wine

An image of an aeroplane
the propeller is rashers of bacon
the wings are of reinforced lard
the tail is made of paperclips
the pilot is a wasp

An image of the painter
with his left hand in a bucket
and his right hand stroking a cat
as he lies in bed
with a stone beneath his head

And all these images
and many others
are arranged like waxworks
in model birdcages
about six inches high.


*SELECTED POEMS, 1994*

HAROLD PINTER

*Cricket at Night*


They are still playing cricket at night
They are playing the game in the dark
They're on guard for a backlash of light

They are losing the ball at long leg
They are trying to learn how the dark
Helps the yorker knock back the off-peg

They are trying to find a new trick
Where the ball moves to darkness from light
They're determined to paint the scene black
But a blackness compounded by white
They are dying to pass a new law
Where blindness is deemed to be sight

They are still playing cricket at night


*THE DISAPPEARED AND OTHER POEMS, 2002*

DAVID MILLER

## An Afternoon with a Circus

An afternoon with a circus:
with dream-owls,
with Chinese shadow-figures,
with a Shepherd of Clouds
for Ringmaster.

And his wife painted
shyly and humbly
but with conviction,
painted and wove
the clear colours and
shapes.

Baobab, they called their son,
the one of indefinite growth,
the one to be lived in, a home,
the one which gives of food
and of water, whose ashes
can be used for salt.

*THE CARYATIDS, 1975*

MICHAEL HENRY

## Boulevard Theatre

After the dancing dogs
'après les chiens qui dansent'
and the topiary of poodles

After the feral tiger feats
and the lion *sans* unicorn
'playing the harp' with his paws

After the Kama Sutra of highwires
Heath Robinsons with a rainbow
and the stale of Spanish Horses

After the night sweats of ammonia
the ripples of pectorals
and eyes glazed and glurrid

After the sawdust rubbed in the nostrils
after the perspiration of canvas
and usherettes with trays of confetti . . .

Boulevards are leafless and bare
last year's leaf worn to a hairnet
and nobody's shadow comes bold.

AFTER THE DANCING DOGS, 2008

CHRIS BECKETT

## The Dog Who Thinks He's a Fish

It's on a plane that Harry tells me about his dog,
a Pointer with the long ears and square muzzle,
the strong, spare body that locks into position
like a well-oiled gun when it's primed to shoot,
except that Harry's dog not only likes to swim
like a labrador fetching ducks, but like a fish,
that is with his head immersed and eyes wide open
staring into the sea, coming up to Harry underwater
and shoving his nose up close, letting out a bark
that sounds like a small thud and sends ropes
of excited bubbles floating to the surface.
Never mind the legs thrashing and the tail trying
its best to wag and steer at the same time,
forget the lack of gills or of any attempt to sieve
a bodyweight of plankton through his teeth,
this is a dog who sees no difference between
himself and fish, enjoying the element of both
and a good shake between the two,
which isn't far removed from me and Harry
knocking back a drink and chattering
like sparrows as our plane takes off.

ENTERING THE TAPESTRY, *ed. Mimi Khalvati and
Graham Fawcett, 2003*

DUNCAN FORBES

## Prisoner of Conscience

Thirteen shiny tins
of John West pink salmon
have been spot-welded, I think,
onto a curved steel wire
to simulate body and spine
of a sockeye salmon leaping
out of the sculptor's mind
into the leasehold air
of a shrine to art and Mammon.

Fish-head and fish-tail
are burnished aluminium.
The eyes of Indian ink
follow you round the room.
If salmon could speak to salmon,
this creature would be
their crucified Statue of Liberty.
By the millennium
perhaps it will stink.

TAKING LIBERTIES, 1993

228

NICKI JACKOWSKA

## Magpie

I always did love the blues
that deepening rasp of throat or string.
We are steeped in blue notes from
the dusk of our mind's penumbra
to the place where a fox might lie
in daylight, shadow-pocked in the land.
She has stitched and shaped him
draws out his stealth in the scratch
and scrape of our pens as they worry the page,
the cloth, tease at particulars; we have known
in this afternoon's abundance, outside & inward
the way a quilt can carry you across
a continent, the breathing of a creature beyond sense.
We have found tense and tension, an architect's fine-tune,
the tucks and knots, tracks and trace of thread
and skein, the age of indigo, the way
that colour shifts and salts the spectrum
nudging up to red and ochre, sending shadows
through the palette, humming, tinting, smouldering,
the seepage of a blue too complex for one day's
inhabiting; we wear our Joseph-coats to better
trawl the length of it, kick it aside, find its disguises.

BEHOLD, 2009

KATE RHODES

## Sun in an Empty Room
*Edward Hopper, 1962*


I would say still, not empty.
The kind of hard American stillness
you come across in hotel lobbies,
in the hour between the porter's last drink
and the kitchen opening at dawn.

Sunlight arrived by 4 a.m., strong enough
to brand its initials on the drab wall –
two hard-edged columns, tall as doorways.
As if you could step straight through
into glory or the heart of summer.

Leaves rail against the locked window
but nature has been evicted.
Light is the sole occupant.
It plans to live here like Greta Garbo,
unphotographed and alone.


REVERSAL, 2005

JANE DURAN

## *In the Paintings of Edward Hopper*

May we stop here?
In the filling station
the meter is at zero.

Up and down the laundered
street – it is guesswork
what goes on
behind the open windows.

A face turns from another face
swept into the glare
a small town
dares to withstand.

The eyes could fill with tears.
A wolf could come from the woods
meaning it.

We sap our strength
raking leaves, over coffee,
in a room for the night
or sitting quietly

till daybreak. Houses
take up their old positions
in the wind.

All at once the looseness of fir trees,
the seemliness of our lives.

*COASTAL, 2005*

RICHARD BERENGARTEN

## Male Figure Playing a Double Flute*
(National Museum, Athens)

In austere polished marble, Orpheus plays,
his flute clamped tight between untiring jaws,
immune to criticism, deaf to praise,
transcending censure, wonder or applause.

With those twin pipes stuck in that chinless face
he played the first tune Asia ever heard,
and smuggled it to Europe out of Thrace:
he plays it now, though we don't hear a word,

His arms are poised like handles of some urn
that held a script which spelt the name divine,
but we who puzzle out its script to learn
that ageless secret, cannot read a line.

The long proud lifted neck, unleashed in leaping
from the four-footed posture of the beast,
signals the world that Europe's soul is sleeping
and mind has not yet dawned upon the East.

Erect, yet legs like haunches, feet like paws,
his thighs primeval tree trunks turned to stone,
bridges from mind's inquiry and earth's laws
to silence that's immortal and alone.

He plays himself: there is no other song
behind those eyes, half closed in ecstasy,
but the same trial through all the ages long,
the erring spirit rising over entropy.

*DOUBLE FLUTE, 1972*

FARZANEH KHOJANDI *translated by* JO SHAPCOTT *and*
NARGUESS FARZAD

## *Flute Player*


Where is the real bazaar?
I want to buy an eyeful of kindness.
I want to dress my soul in hyperbole.
There's a merchant who brings me
a whole spectrum of leaping colour
from the city of desires.
But here at the bazaar at Khojand,
faces are sour, talk is hot
and I long for the cool sweets of Tabriz.
Where is the real bazaar?
The flute-player tells me:
come with your ears used to insults,
and listen to the light recite a prayer to the dark.
Open your eyes used to pale shame
and see the beauty of Truth.
Where is the real bazaar?
The flute player is there
calling my heart towards his hat
full of old change, but not a single pearl,
and since I am the jewel in the teardrop
I must go.


POEMS, 2008 *in association with the Poetry Translation Centre*

EDWARD DORN

## On First Looking into Shakespeare's Folios just after Christmas 1998, at the New British Library

It's not a state secret
That E mail is not written.
Why is this when ordinarily
Good writers are writing it?
The reason is that E mail
Is inherently bad—in and of itself
And if the most elegant and pains-
Taking care and craft were taken
With its execution the result
Would be inelegant, ugly, cheap
Clap trap and disgusting.
E mail just doesn't think
Nor does it "write."
A message that cannot wait 3 days
Is probably not at all urgent
Or worthy of delivery.
We know this
Because the messages of great importance
Have no standardized delivery rate
Whether by horse, human runner, or the
Flash of mirror from Queribus to Puylaurens.
A cable can be handed to you
With a flourish, terse language
Pasted on crisp paper—
What an occasion!

Of course that is why it's ascendant
And will probably be final—unless
When the lights go out the goose quill
Hath another day.

*DERELICT AIR: FROM COLLECTED OUT, 2015*

John Lawrence, *The Actor*, from *Light Unlocked:*
*Christmas Card Poems* (2005)

ALAN BROWNJOHN

*The Arrows*


They point in a line across the foot of the page
To a kiss that ends the letter in the farthest
Right-hand corner.

Most of the arrows believe, 'She will see the kiss
Without our help, why should we all line up
To take our turn at pointing out the kiss?

'We could refer to another place or object,
Directions for someone actually *unsure*
About where he is going.'

But the wisest of the arrows addresses
The rest of them saying, 'If we took off our heads
And straightened them, and crossed them with our bodies

We could one by one become kisses ourselves in turn,
And the thousands more in the queue off the left-hand edge
Would know they have something to wait for.'


*LUDBROOKE & OTHERS, 2010*

236

ANTHONY THWAITE

## Arabic Script

Like a spider through ink, someone says, mocking: see it
Blurred on the news-sheets or in neon lights
And it suggests an infinitely plastic, feminine
Syllabary, all the diacritical dots and dashes
Swimming together like a shoal of minnows,
Purposive yet wayward, a wavering measure
Danced over meaning, obscuring vowels and breath.
But at Sidi Kreibish, among the tombs,
Where skulls lodge in the cactus roots,
The pink claws breaking headstone, cornerstone,
Each fleshy tip thrusting to reach the light,
Each spine a hispid needle, you see the stern
Edge of the language, Kufic, like a scimitar
Curved in a lash, a flash of consonants
Such as swung out of Medina that day
On the long flog west, across ruins and flaccid colonials,
A swirl of black flags, white crescents, a language of swords.

SELECTED POEMS 1956–1996, 1997

KIT WRIGHT

## Riddle*

I go through the wood in silence
and come out on to the snow
where I leave my prints
though I have no footsteps,
where I speak your heart
though I cannot breathe.

THE NEW EXETER BOOK OF RIDDLES,
ed. Kevin Crossley-Holland and Lawrence Sail, 1999

EDWIN MORGAN

## from *Thirteen Ways of Looking at Rillie**

11

Friend of language!
from the Word on Patmos
to highest-kilted metaphors
of critical discourse,
Rillie told me how
his ears lit up
when he read in a paper
about two fossil fish
newly named in China:
Haikouichthys
(daddy of the lampreys)
Myllokunmingia
(gaffer of all hagfish)
snuffed in the Lower Cambrian
sleeping till now.
Be proud of your names
you ancient creatures!
You are not forgotten,
five hundred million years
a flick of the tail
in the ocean of all.

THIRTEEN WAYS OF LOOKING AT RILLIE, 2006

PAUL MULDOON

## A Dent*

*In memory of Michael Allen*

The height of one stall at odds with the next in your grandfather's byre
where cattle allowed themselves to speak only at Yule
gave but little sense of why you taught us to admire
the capacity of a three-legged stool

to take pretty much everything in its stride,
even the card-carrying Crow who let out a war-whoop
now your red pencil was poised above my calf-hide
manuscript like a graip above a groop.

The depth of a dent in the flank of your grandfather's cow
from his having leaned his brow
against it morning and night

for twenty years of milking by hand
gave but little sense of how distant is the land
on which you had us set our sights.

*SONGS AND SONNETS, 2012*

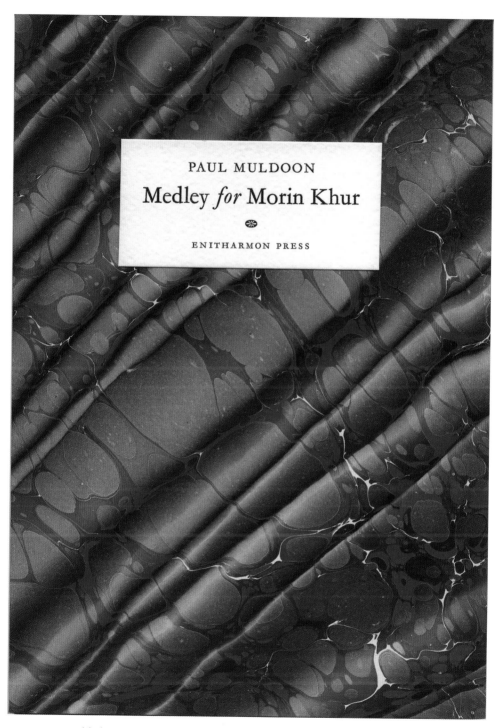

Marbled-wrappered cover of Paul Muldoon's letterpress-printed chapbook
*Medley for Morin Khur* (2005)

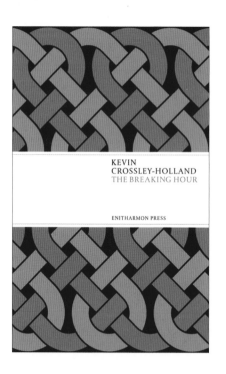

KEVIN
CROSSLEY-HOLLAND
THE BREAKING HOUR

ENITHARMON PRESS

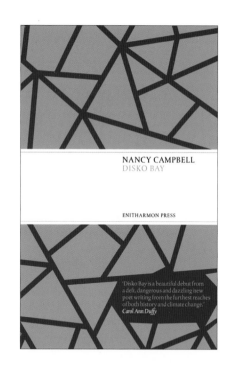

NANCY CAMPBELL
DISKO BAY

ENITHARMON PRESS

'Disko Bay is a beautiful debut from
a deft, dangerous and dazzling new
poet writing from the furthest reaches
of both history and climate change.'
*Carol Ann Duffy*

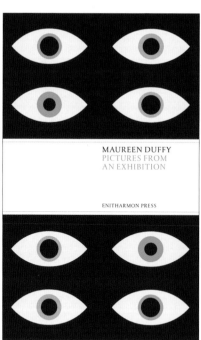

MAUREEN DUFFY
PICTURES FROM
AN EXHIBITION

ENITHARMON PRESS

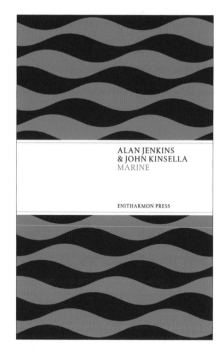

ALAN JENKINS
& JOHN KINSELLA
MARINE

ENITHARMON PRESS

Series design for 2015 paperbacks

THE ANCIENT MARINER

DAVID JONES

EDITED BY THOMAS DILWORTH

ENITHARMON

Dust-jacket of David Jones's *The Ancient Mariner* (2006)

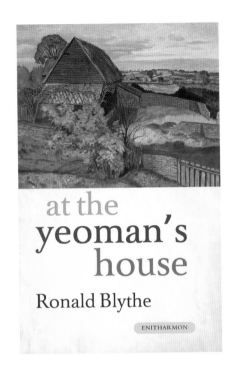

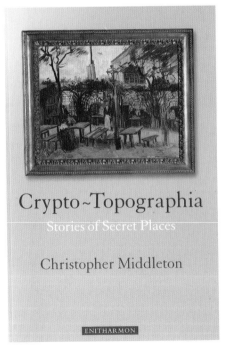

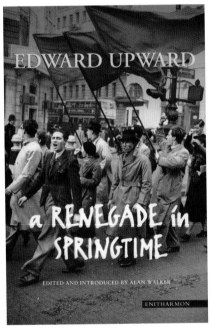

A selection of prose books

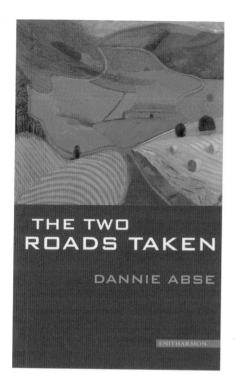
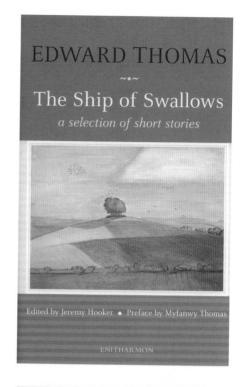

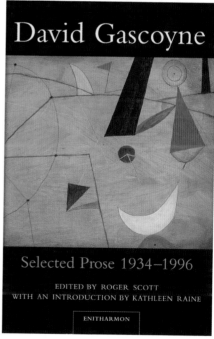

A selection of prose books

# Branch-Lines
## Edward Thomas
## and Contemporary Poetry

EDITED BY

GUY CUTHBERTSON & LUCY NEWLYN

FOREWORD BY ANDREW MOTION
AFTERWORD BY MICHAEL LONGLEY

ENITHARMON

Dust-jacket of *Branch-Lines* (new edition, 2014)

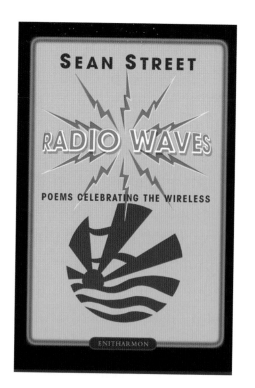

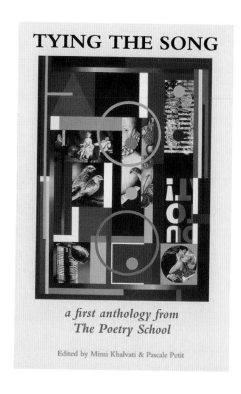

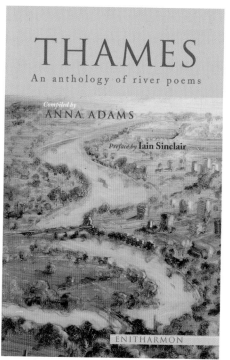

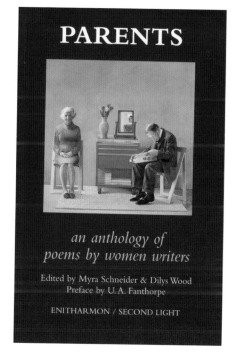

A selection of anthologies

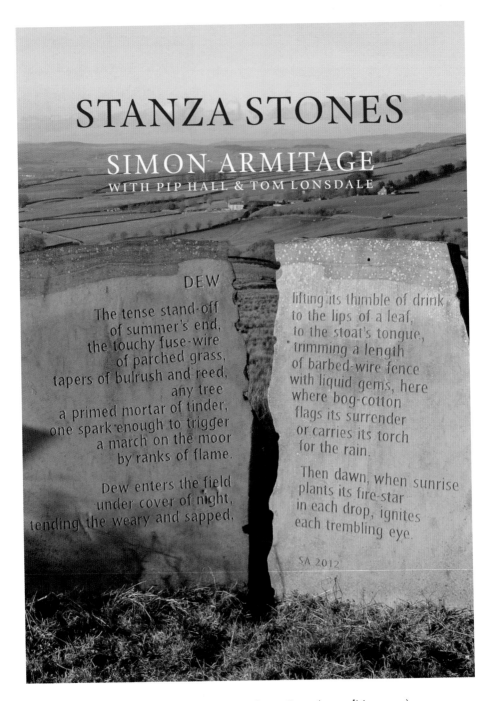

# STANZA STONES

## SIMON ARMITAGE
### WITH PIP HALL & TOM LONSDALE

### DEW

The tense stand-off
of summer's end,
the touchy fuse-wire
of parched grass,
tapers of bulrush and reed,
any tree
a primed mortar of tinder,
one spark enough to trigger
a march on the moor
by ranks of flame.

Dew enters the field
under cover of night,
tending the weary and sapped,

lifting its thimble of drink
to the lips of a leaf,
to the stoat's tongue,
trimming a length
of barbed-wire fence
with liquid gems, here
where bog-cotton
flags its surrender
or carries its torch
for the rain.

Then dawn, when sunrise
plants its fire-star
in each drop, ignites
each trembling eye.

SA 2012

Dust-jacket of Simon Armitage's *Stanza Stones* (new edition, 2017),
showing the lettercarver Pip Hall's 'Dew' stone

SEAMUS HEANEY

*The City*

i

Water-slicked hair already wafer-dry
By the start of class, he'd arrive
Wrist-deep in the perpetual soutane,

Still worrying bits of refectory breakfast
Between his teeth, the satin lining
Of his tossed-back shoulder-cape

The only thing agleam in the usual
He was inured to: us there in our desks
Observing silence, him readying himself,

Then the pause and the unsighed sigh
Before the sighed one, 'Och boys,
I wish it were Book Six.'

ii

But Livy it was instead, in 'selections'
Selected further by our man of sighs,
Resigned to it but sad it couldn't be

Hexameter verse, even that which urged
Conquest and imperium on Rome,
Whom to crush, to spare, to pacify.

Yet everywhere in that unremitting prose
Behind the augury and oratory
And carnage, one word shone

Like a Virgilian moon, the feminine-gendered,
Argent, birch-barked *urbs*
Risen over chalk-groined *Alba Longa*.

iii

Not that Homeric light has not been shed
On 'the city', our Illium now,
Your gate the one where Priam creeps back in

With Hector's body, mine the one
Aeneas slips out from with Anchises,
Fathers and sons

The pair of us, grandfathers too,
More pastoral/lyrical than epical,
Inclined to scry the gloom for what might gleam

As when a seal's head rose and streamed and shone
For four of us, walking the harbour wall
In the sealight of Ardglass.

*LOVE POET, CARPENTER: MICHAEL LONGLEY AT SEVENTY*,
ed. Robin Robertson, 2009

MICHAEL SCHMIDT

## from *The Love of Strangers*

It wasn't snowing but it should have been.
You were an old man, nine months from the grave.
Your hand was very dry and very hot
And large, as I recall (I was a boy,
Fourteen years at most, I led you round
Part of the school, your guide; you seemed to listen).
That night you read in a slow, dismissive voice
That left the words like notes on staves hung in the air,
No longer yours, but part of memory –
You talked about Miss Dickinson of Amherst
And said aloud the eight lines of her poem
'The heart asks pleasure first'.  And from that night
I've known the poem word-perfect, part of me.

I think you let more lines free into language
And memory with your rusty, lonely voice
Than any other poet of our age.
It must have been like freeing doves
And watching them go off to neighbouring cotes
Or into the low clouds of your New Hampshire
Knowing they'll meet no harm, that they'll survive
Long after the hand that freed them has decayed.

Those lines are wise in rhythm and they lead
Into a clapboard dwelling, or a field,
Or lives that prey upon the land and one another,
Or the big country where we both were children.

AN ENITHARMON ANTHOLOGY FOR ALAN CLODD, 1990

JANE GRIFFITHS

## Legend Has It*

it was the answer to a prayer after
years of careful construction on the weights
and pulleys of borrowed syntax, lines

of thought running like the black bands
and fretwork of Victorian gothic
to display a niche, a clause, a window

embrasure capped with periods of perfect
equilibrium and the loadbearing mind
countersunk in its shadow:
                              suddenly the poem

sufficient unto itself as the long minute's
view when a train pauses between stations,
the country one part earth to six parts air

and the white house in its clean timber
frame clear and open as if it stood alone
and unlooked-for. Or so they say.

BRANCH-LINES: EDWARD THOMAS AND
CONTEMPORARY POETRY, ed. Guy Cuthbertson
and Lucy Newlyn, 2007

YANNIS RITSOS *versions by* DAVID HARSENT

## Blocked

Clouds on the face of the mountain, stones on the ground,
birds in the air. He walks a little way,
then turns back. The valley's a bed of thistles. In the window
of the only house, a blue jug. Who is to blame for all this?
The poem shrugs him off.
Words are defined by what they dare not say.

*IN SECRET, 2012*

JOHN WIENERS

## A Poem for Tea Heads

I sit in Lees.      At 11:40 PM with
Jimmy the pusher.  He teaches me
Ju Ju.
       Hot on the table before us
shrimp foo yong, rice and mushroom
chow yuke.
       Up the street under the wheels
of a strange car is his stash —The ritual.
We make it.     And have made it.
For months now together after midnight.
Soon I know the fuzz will inter-
rupt will arrest Jimmy and
I shall be placed on probation.
         The poem
does not lie to us.  We lie under its
law, alive in the glamour of this hour
able to enter into the sacred places
of his dark people, who carry secrets
glassed in their eyes and hide words
     under the roofs of their mouth.

SUPPLICATION: SELECTED POEMS, ed. Joshua Beckman,
C. A. Conrad and Robert Dewhurst, 2015

CHRISTOPHER MIDDLETON

*Elegy of the Flowing Touch*


Almost anywhere there's a poem lying around
Waiting for someone to lift it up, dust it off,

For instance, the argument with a neighbour
About a large dog: was it a German Shepherd

Or a mutt?  Would it jump into the sea hereabouts
To save a child, if a child went overboard?

The argument was conducted in civilized terms,
But we stood in the street, there were distractions,

In spite of which we both felt for the crux:
Does a dog have a will capable of the Good?

Insistent as I was that, however eagerly it swam
Toward the child, a mutt, being untrained,

Might forget the good it had set out to do,
I was brooding on something else – the dignity

Of the dog, whatever it was, standing as we had seen it
There on the prow of a small rubber boat;

That figurehead of a dog, did it know
How dignified it might look to the likes of us?

Who cared if it jumped into the water?
Who cared if it collared a floundering child?

And under the brooding lurked, not yet material,
A poem scheming to coax into focus a local image –

Ten dinghies fluttering tiny peppermint sails,
Each dinghy a nest with two children in it,

Strung out on a cord behind the rubber mother boat,
All the children laughing, waving, and feeling free,

The bursts of song from the children's throats,
And before them, gold against an oceanic blue,

The figurehead dog, ears pinned back by the wind,
His attention to it all, and a great joy in his jowls.

Even then, the scene: and the poem would pivot
On breathlessness, a moment of suspense.

How, it would say, as the procession of dinghies
Headed away from the coast and out to sea,

Either their voices had passed out of earshot,
Or else the children were learning fear.

The silence now as they skim over the water.
The blue of a ravening deep underneath them.


TWENTY TROPES FOR DOCTOR DARK, 2000

MAXAMED XAASHI DHAMAC 'GAARRIYE'
*translated by* W.N. HERBERT *and* MARTIN ORWIN

# from *Seer*

When she brought me up, Biliso said,
'If a poem is a farm
then how things truly are, that's water;
the best words for the best thoughts,
that's how it begins.
Justice is your only compost,
life itself is what you hoe:
just squeeze truth from what happens
and in its own time it will sprout.'

'Whether a poem brings forth seeds
depends on how it's tended and by whom –
the spot in which it's planted;
depending on who needs it and for what
its husk is hulled or boiled.'

'A poem is the measure for
that trek beneath the draining sun
each generation adds to;
when you have to stand and fight
it shows you where to point the gun.'

'It guides you like a conch shell horn,
the call of the large camel bell;
it is the words' own bugle.
It is the finest matting, woven for a bride,
the one the song calls "Refuser of poor suitors".
It's not sold for coppers,

it's not for praising the powerful;
to put a price on it, any price,
cheapens it and is forbidden.'

'It's riding bareback on an unbroken horse –
you don't hobble its heels.
Those who fear for their hides
and won't ride without a saddle,
those lacking in the craft, can't get near this:
lies have nothing to do with it.
Poetry is a woman you do not betray,
to abuse her beauty is a sin.'

POEMS, 2008 *in association with the Poetry Translation Centre*

TED HUGHES

## Little Whale Song
*for Charles Causley*


What do they think of themselves
With their global brains –
The tide-power voltage illumination
Of those brains?  Their X-ray all-dimension

Grasp of this world's structures, their brains budded
Clone replicas of the electron world
Lit and re-imagining the world,
Perfectly-tuned receivers and perceivers,

Each one a whole tremulous world
Feeling through the world?  What
Do they make of each other?

'We are beautiful.  We stir

Our self-colour in the pot of colours
Which is the world.  At each
Tail-stroke we deepen
Our being into the world's lit substance,

And our joy into the world's
Spinning bliss, and our peace
Into the world's floating, plumed peace.'

Their body-tons, echo-chambered,

Amplify the whisper
Of currents and airs, of sea-peoples

And planetary manoeuvres,
Of seasons, of shores, and of their own

Moon-lifted incantation, as they dance
Through the original world-drama –
In which they perform, as from the beginning,
The Royal House.
                    The loftiest, spermiest

Passions, the most delicate pleasures,
The noblest characters, the most godlike
Oceanic presence and poise,
The most terrible fall.


POEMS FOR CHARLES CAUSLEY, 1982

JOHN HEATH-STUBBS

## The Heron

An image remembered from boyhood – glimpsed
From a moving train: a pool,
Or else a brook which must have run perforce
Beside the tracks, and a heron standing,
Not in his grey stillness,
Watching the waters for his prey – but all in motion,
As he tries to get into his snaking gullet
A flapping, white-bellied, obstinate cuss of a fish.

BIRDS RECONVENED, 1980

MAUREEN DUFFY

## Cows Crossing

Round the corner I brake, the tarmac ahead
become a comber of cows, a flash flood of flesh
a surge of fluid black and white boulders
their legs gaunt trestles for the bagpipe
of cream that threatens to topple them
shoehorns skittering on their own slurry
yet whose gait's somehow graceful, measured
two by two like schoolgirls in a crocodile
or eternal children holding arms or hands
with ribbons in their forty-year-old shingles
and draggletail print frocks, out for a treat.

They cross with the sideways seesaw of hammocks.
Sometimes a head turns to look at my throb of car
checking the flow a moment, then wedges forward again
to follow, knowing I have no answers
just that twice a day she must cross from one
mud-puddled field to another as long as she lives
blessedly not foreseeing as I do the bolt
for captives, the pithing rod: Aditi
wetnurse to us all come down to this ponderous
pendulous presence on the road that too briefly
breaks my journey with her gangling epiphany
momentary damascene incised on a grey morning
piercing, pierced.

FAMILY VALUES, 2008

RUTH PITTER

## Swifts

Low over the warm roof of an old barn,
Down in a flash to the water, up and away with a cry
And a wild swoop and a sharp turn
And a fever of life under a thundery sky,
So they go over, so they go by.

And high and high and high in the diamond light,
Soaring and crying in sunshine when heaven is bare,
With the pride of life in their strong flight
And a rapture of love to lift them and carry them there,
High and high in the diamond air.

And away with the summer, away like the spirit of glee,
Flashing and calling, strong on the wing, and wild in their play,
With a high cry to the high sea,
And a heart for the south, a heart for the diamond day,
So they go over, so go away.

COLLECTED POEMS, 1990

ANNE STEVENSON

## Bird in Hand

The tiny wren perched on your hand
could be a key.  Then
somewhere should be the door
that with a bird-shaped key-hole
cut by wind into stiff sand
must fit that needle beak and pinhead eye,
that tail's armed signal to the clamped wings,
Fly! Spring the lock! Lift the floor
from the earth, the roof from the sky,
and with a fanfare of trills
– no trumpets, no veils –
reveal the Quaker heaven where this bird sings.

*IN THE ORCHARD, 2016*

Gwen Raverat, *Cambridge Autumn 1* and *Cambridge Autumn 2*, block
cuts of 1934 from Frances Cornford's *Selected Poems* (1996)

JOHN MOLE

## To a Blackbird at First Light

Clasp whatever branch you may land on
and, just for the joy of it, from a full throat
sing, before flight, of yet another season
coming into leaf. Let every grace note
seed where it falls, and the point-blank
not-to-be-born-again remorselessness of dawn
receive your gift. As if there were God to thank
for this, as if not randomly thrown
but scattered for a purpose, may your song
resist interpretation much as beauty does
the suffering it causes. So let the branch be strong
on which you chance to land, a melodious
accidental choice, no giving way,
and sing there for the joy of it, the pure joy.

*THE POINT OF LOSS, 2011*

GEORGE MacBETH

*Owl*


is my favourite. Who flies
like a nothing through the night,
who-whoing. Is a feather
duster in leafy corners ring-a-rosy-ing
boles of mice. Twice

you hear him call. Who
is he looking for? You hear
him hoovering over the floor
of the wood. O would you be gold
rings in the driving skull

if you could? Hooded and
vulnerable by the winter suns
owl looks. Is the grain of bark
in the dark. Round beaks are at
work in the pellety nest,

resting. Owl is an eye
in the barn. For a hole
in the trunk owl's blood
is to blame. Black talons in the
petrified fur! Cold walnut hands

on the case of the brain! In the reign
of the chicken owl comes like
a god. Is a goad in
the rain to the pink eyes,
dripping. For a meal in the day

flew, killed, on the moor. Six
mouths are the seed of his
arc in the season. Torn meat
from the sky. Owl lives
by the claws of his brain. On the branch

in the sever of the hand's
twigs owl is a backward look.
Flown wind in the skin. Fine
rain in the bones. Owl breaks
like the day. Am an owl, am an owl.

SELECTED POEMS, ed. Anthony Thwaite, 2002

CHRISTOPHER WISEMAN

## Cod Fishing

Cold November nights are best
With the high tide whipped
By a razor wind, the waves
Exploding like shells on the rocks.

Like tonight.
The fingers can hardly grip
To put the lugworm on
To control the huge cast

Over the seaweed and rocks
Eighty yards with luck
Right into the big combers.
You can't see where it goes.

And then it's waiting,
The bell on the rod whirring
In the gale, hands useless
In pockets, face frozen,

The white sea in the blackness
And some white stars
Between low cruising clouds
And the tide getting round you

And the rod-tip jerking
But only with the wind
With vibration from the breakers
Though the numb heart jumps.

Likely as not this is all
You'll ever get.
Likely as not this is all
You could ever stand.

*THE UPPER HAND, 1981*

Erica Sail, *Fishing Boat at Beer*, drawing from Lawrence Sail's
*Songs of the Darkness* (2010)

ADAM THORPE

## Sea Otter

Of course we were always meant
to watch this slicked-down head

appear and reappear in the Sound's
rocky inlet beyond the lane's verge

from our hired cottage on Harris
overlooking the sky's meltdown

at dusk. But whether it's feeding, playing
or simply luxuriating in the violet

gloom and glitter of the sea
after its den's blind room

we have no idea, knowing
next to nothing about any creature.

It vanishes only to be repeatedly spotted –
allotted half-an-hour of our lives

before the excitement palls
and the binoculars are left

on the sill, no longer fought for. What
doesn't, in the end, become familiar

all round, however strange or fine?
I wish that sea-otter's amazement was mine.

LOVE POET, CARPENTER: MICHAEL LONGLEY
AT SEVENTY, ed. Robin Robertson, 2009

MARIO PETRUCCI

i rather love


not things but
what lies behind
these the way a year

is sometimes glimpsed
past ear of corn or
december

come
out of blue to
one who knew only

sun – perhaps such
are best unsaid
so all might

speak of
corn & sky or
strip decembers

down to black-
scaffold
trees

where
life sings &
sings to death each

silenced thing


*i tulips*, 2010

PAULINE STAINER

*Our Lady of Indigo*


Desultory blue –
the weight of water,
scarcely a blue animal
on the ark.

Blue to conjure with –
fields of blue alfalfa
making the moonlight
something else.

Profound blue –
the master of the blue crucifix
opening his throat
to her thin-blue milk.


*LIGHT UNLOCKED: CHRISTMAS CARD POEMS,*
ed. *Kevin Crossley-Holland and Lawrence Sail,* 2005

RAINER MARIA RILKE *translated by* MARTYN CRUCEFIX

# *Duino Elegies*
## from *The First Elegy*

It's true enough, of course, no longer to live
on earth is strange, to abandon customs
barely mastered yet, not to interpret roses
and other auspicious things, not give them meaning
in a human future.  No longer to be as we have
always been, in those endlessly anxious hands –
to leave even our name behind us as a child
leaves off playing with a broken toy.  Strange,
no longer to know desires desired – strange
to witness the involvement of all things lost
suddenly, each drifting away singly into space.
And truly, to be dead is hard, so full of making
up lost ground, till little by little we find
a trace of eternity.  Yet, the living are wrong
to draw such distinctions so clearly:
angels (it is said) are often never quite sure
whether they pass among the living or the dead,
since through both these realms, and forever,
eternity's flood tumbles all the ages and in both
their cries are drowned out by its roar.

In the end, the young-dead do not need us:
they are weaned off the earth mildly as a child
will outgrow the mother's breast.  But we,
who long for such great mysteries, we, for whom
sorrow is often the path on which we progress –
*can* we exist without them?  Is the old myth
really nonsense?  The one about the mourning of Linus,

how music first broke on the barren wilderness;
how, in the startled space left gaping by the loss
of a boy like a god, emptiness rang as never before
with what holds us rapt, comforts now and can help.

*DUINO ELEGIES, 2006*

John Lawrence, *Hyacinths,* illustration from
*Light Unlocked: Christmas Card Poems* (2005)

DAVID CONSTANTINE

## Hyacinths

The tortoise earth seems to have stopped dead.
Certainly the trees are dead, their limbs
Are broken, we can hear them clattering.
It must be about the midpoint.  Last year
At this time you knelt for the hyacinths.

You brought them in like bread, in fired bowls,
From secret ovens of darkness.  Three or four rooms
Soon had a column and a birth.  Pictures show
The crib shining similarly
When Christ flowered from Mary the bulb.

The Kings stand warming their hands on the light.
Their gifts are nothing by comparison.
I suppose they feared that without some miracle,
Without the light and the bread of hyacinths,
The earth would never nudge forward out of the dark.

LIGHT UNLOCKED: CHRISTMAS CARD POEMS,
ed. Kevin Crossley-Holland and Lawrence Sail, 2005

CORSINO FORTES *translated by* SEAN O'BRIEN
*and* DANIEL HAHN

## When Morning Breaks

Oh when
Oh when the morning breaks
And the night becomes more night
When the morning breaks
With its feet on the ground
And the earth in its heart
When blood flows from the body
Like a tree with open arms
And the seed shouts from the rock
Like a green-mouthed drum
And from that sound
That warrior's blood
Mouths are born
    centred mouths
    torn mouths
In the wheel of the sun

Oh when the morning breaks
Without hanging its despair
On the flag of the door
Without lighting torches
On the donkeys' tails
To bring wrecks
Without shipwrecks
On the people's tongues
Then the desperate sea – very high –
    Bravo!
Will come to break on Praia Grande
On its fat sinful arms

And the sea will come
In its luxury
In its grandeur
Showing its mast
On the heart's rough seas
Its white map
Drawn on the soul
Will come to drink in my colonized tongue
All the history of my ultramarine blood

Oh when the morning breaks
And Christ descends from his dwelling
And comes
To the right arm of Monte Cara
With the handle of his hoe
And his drill shorts
Barefoot
With a split finger
And sits down
At our round cooking-stone
With no rain in his hand
No weakness in his blood
No crow in his heart

Oh when
Oh when the morning breaks


POEMS, 2008 *in association with the*
*Poetry Translation Centre*

MARTYN CRUCEFIX

## Scraps
*for Thomas*


All I can stomach of cathedrals
these days is the detail.
Not the stand-back-and-gawp
that grows too rich for me –
the wide-angle too much,
the whole too vertiginous to please.

A cherub's backside is good to see.
His little pigeon-winged shoulders
fine for me – to be truthful
exactly the kind of thing
worth getting up to closely
if I'm on church ground at all.

Or arches. Or terracotta tiles.
Or the dusty glimmer of brass.
No more than a looker-on,
I walk with my six-year-old son,
confidently thinking I'm done
with the absence of faith

although something remains –
a single thread slipped the shears
passing on from me to him
becomes clear as we push
through the door's polished grain
slap-bang into the blurt

of ring-tone scraps, the street's
flagrant whine, its rapid fade
and sudden brake-light, the smash
and grab of shop-wisdom . . .
As one – as the touched horns
of a snail – we shrink in.

So this is what I hope for him:
a stronger belief than I knew,
that the solitary man
in his quietude need not
be scorned and ridiculed,
need not have plagued so bitterly

my boyhood – the guts
to see whole cultures have anchored
high tide in retreat,
though others deride it
and more: the few details I managed
in the cathedral before.

*HURT, 2010*

HUBERT MOORE

## Crossing the Church

Some seem born to it.  They could cross
the gleaming track from the nave to the altar
blindfold.

Look, no hands even.  Now they're squaring
their shoulders eastwards, gravely inclining
their heads;

and now they're over, strolling off amidst pews,
leaving one at least of us standing
helpless

as ever to help the children we were,
who anyway couldn't be helped,
born

trespassers, laying our ears
to the cold steel of the track, hearing
the rail

singing the song that we hoped for,
five miles off, centuries still
for us,                              .

knees bare on the flinty stone,
heads where the wheels would be rolling –
then scrambling safely across.

ROLLING STOCK, 1991

NEIL CURRY

## León

This, in my eyes, is the great cathedral.
Proof that actuality need not always
Be the impoverishment of what is possible.

In its Gothic fragility it holds back
From Baroque's magniloquent contempt for tact.

I sit and watch the shadows of the nesting storks.
Like holy ghosts, they rise and fall
Behind the stained-glass windows of the choir.

With three rose-windows, and over two
Hundred storied and decorated panes,
It sometimes seems that there's more glass than stone.

But late of an afternoon, when the sun
Rings in through these golds, these greens, these reds,
And through this lapis blue, it can feel

As though it is neither glass nor stone,
But the light itself that sustains it all.

*WALKING TO SANTIAGO, 1992*

JOHN WHITWORTH

## What It Isn't

Old evidences of decay
Still linger in the mind
And little that you do or say
Seems apposite or kind.
You preach more often than you pray,
You lose more than you find.

> It isn't what you take away.
> It's what you leave behind.

You win so rarely when you play;
The players rob you blind.
You owe what you can never pay;
The cheques remain unsigned.
Your night encroaches on your day;
The exits all are mined.

> It isn't what you take away.
> It's what you leave behind.

All thoughts that you permit to stray
Are sexually inclined,
Indifferently straight or gay,
You chew them to the rind.
There has to be a better way
to deal with humankind.

> It isn't what you take away.
> It's what you leave behind.

Say yea or nay – to go or stay,
To scatter or to bind?
You're wary of the ricochet
And cut what won't unwind.
You tighten up the tourniquet
And wait to be assigned.

> *It isn't what you take away,*
> *It's never what you take away,*
> *It's what you leave behind.*


GIRLIE GANGS, 2012

SHEILA WINGFIELD

## Hope

Hope or so I fancy
Is bright-haired
And nimble

Tufts of seapinks
Come up in her footprints
And where her fingers
Touch a wall
Heart's-ease grows
From the crevice

If she pauses a moment
In a family graveyard
Then blue bugle
Will cover the ground

For all her youth
She is old as humanity
And none else
Long ago
Could have refreshed the soul
In shadowy
Deep-layered Lebanon

War and blight
All known miseries
Yap at her heels

But she keeps ahead

COLLECTED POEMS 1938–1983, 1983

JACK CLEMO

## Sufficiency

Yes, I might well grow tired
Of slighting flowers all day long,
Of making my song
Of the mud in the kiln, of the wired
Poles on the clay-dump; but where
Should I find my personal pulse of prayer
If I turned from the broken, scarred
And unkempt land, the hard
Contours of dogma, colourless hills?
Is there a flower that thrills
Like frayed rope? Is there grass
That cools like gravel, and are there streams
Which murmur as clay-silt does that Christ redeems?
I have not heard of any, so I trace
The writings on bruised iron and purged clay face:
'Young son of man, be strong,
For as My dower is, so shall be your song.
There is no weariness for you,
For I will let you view
In a human flower the soft warm growth:
Her tidal sap has touched the soil of both
The real worlds that you scan,
And thus shall make you man.
In the heights you shall hymn but Godhead grim and grey;
In the depths you shall hymn but clay.'

SELECTED POEMS, 2015

285

ANTHONY THWAITE

# Movements

As ice keeps the shape of the bowl
after the bowl is broken,
and the pad in the mud is sure of the bird's sign,
and the bruise on the skin is taken
as a mark of the blood underneath troubled and shaken,
so is the shape of the invisible soul.

As the current wavers and suddenly changes,
plucked by the wind, which no one has ever seen,
and leaves shaken above turn again and again
from white, then to grey, to black, to green,
and their branches fret above from now to then,
so the door between *then* and *now* shifts on its hinges.

As the mist in the headlights lifts and comes down again,
marking a move in the weather we did not know,
and the river rises with only a flurry of snow
melting under a warmth we could not see,
nothing is sure, nothing can ever stay,
so much is the one thing sure, as sure now as then.

A MOVE IN THE WEATHER, 2003

TOMAS TRANSTRÖMER *versions by* ROBIN ROBERTSON

## Solitude (1)

I was nearly killed here, one night in February.
My car shivered, and slewed sideways on the ice,
right across into the other lane. The slur of traffic
came at me with their lights.

My name, my girls, my job, all
slipped free and were left behind, smaller and smaller,
further and further away. I was nobody:
a boy in a playground, suddenly surrounded.

The headlights of the oncoming cars
bore down on me as I wrestled the wheel through a slick
of terror, clear and slippery as egg-white.
The seconds grew and grew – making more room for me –
stretching huge as hospitals.

I almost felt that I could rest
and take a breath
before the crash.

Then something caught: some helpful sand
or a well-timed gust of wind. The car
snapped out of it, swinging back across the road.
A signpost shot up and cracked, with a sharp clang,
spinning away in the darkness.

And it was still. I sat back in my seat-belt
and watched someone tramp through the whirling snow
to see what was left of me.

*THE DELETED WORLD, 2006*

287

NICKY RICE

*Dreams*


I think of them as thin,
almost two-dimensional, a pack of cards
dealing themselves in a mad game with no rules
and they hold all the aces.
It's sheer chance.  No way of telling

which one will show its face.
Sometimes the certainty of homecoming,
the kisses, the made fortune.
Or the disgrace, the nakedness in the market-place,
the gold coins that dissolve in daylight.

It's the joker you have to watch.
He's a sly fox.  He'll smile
into your eyes and then suddenly undo the catch,
letting out the casualties,
the maimed with their terrible amputations.

And they all cheat quite shamelessly,
shuffling memories, getting the addition wrong.
The sea successfully covers its dead.  The heather
blows on the headland, safe anchorage in sight.
Then you awaken and it is grey, grey.

One day they may detach themselves, float up into daylight.
Strange to meet one at noon and not know the difference.
But at least I'll sleep well,
my mind a no man's land,
a bony theatre full of darkness.


COMING UP TO MIDNIGHT, 1994

KATHLEEN RAINE

## Storm-Stayed

Holy, holy holy is the light of day
The gray cloud, the storm wind, the cold sea,
Holy, holy the snow in the mountain,
Holy the stone, the dry heather, the stunted tree,
Holy the heron and the hoodie, holy
The leaf and the rain,
The cold wind and the cold wave, cold light of day
And the turning of earth from night into morning,
Holy this place where I am,
The last house, it may be,
Before the wind, the shelterless sky, the unbounded sea.

*THE OVAL PORTRAIT AND OTHER POEMS, 1977*

RONALD BLYTHE

## Holy Mr Herbert

Holy Mr Herbert, breathing his native air,
Sang a song to Jesus on the Border line,
A boy's song, an early song which went unheard.
Only the linnets listened as it rose and fell.
'We will hear you later, George',
His grown-up brothers said.

Holy Mr Herbert, breathing bad Cambridge air,
Was seized by the fenny ague which lived in that town.
But still he sang a song to Jesus in his clear voice,
For young singers know that they have donkey's years ahead,
And no time to keep.

Holy Mr Herbert, tall and straight and grand,
Sang his Matins in a fallen aisle,
Showed ploughmen and gipsy boys into the best pews,
Wore the cleanest robes, wed his cousin Jane
And galloped into Salisbury every Thursday
To sing with the Singing Men.

Holy Mr Herbert dined on nuts and skim,
Laid a place for Jesus where they could hear each other talk.
Passed him the bread and wine, got thinner
And thinner from the fenny ague, wrote a lot of words,
Then left his living so that he could be everywhere.

For this is what happens to singers, birds or men,
They turn into a tune which hangs around till
Kingdom come. Holy Mr Herbert had a lute, the best words,
A short life, rang his own bell, was properly liturgical
– and quite brilliant, they say.

*DECADAL, 2015*

ANNA ROBINSON

## Agnus

Lamb, I have seen you from trains.
I have seen you as I walked through fields.
You looked back at me, raised
your left hoof towards me in a delicate way.
Lamb, I have found your winter curls
by the roadside, on thorns and on barbed wire.

Lamb, who exalts what the world gets wrong,
its failings, its struggles, honourable lamb
feel for us.

Lamb, all winter I wear black to absorb the sun.
Red is not as good as this. It is only for inside.
Lamb, my mother had a dream,
the whole family lived separately in sheds
in the back yard. It was dark and cold.
When we went to find each other, we weren't there.

Lamb, who exalts what the world gets wrong,
heals wounds, smoothes troubles, loving lamb
feel for us.

Lamb, these derelict testaments are stained.
They're cased in walls of clay. We cannot reach them.
We are damp and raucous, our marsh overgrown.
The trees under our pavements are dead. The stairs,
by which you left to sail up river, lead nowhere.
Lamb, why do we fear ourselves?

Lamb, who exalts what the world gets wrong,
crowns hags, creates doubt, fragrant lamb
give us peace.

*THE FINDERS OF LONDON, 2010*

JOHN WIENERS

## The Blind See only this World
### (A Christmas Card)


Today the Lamb of God arrives in the mail
above the Cross, beside the Handsome Sailor
                                  from Russia
in his turtleneck sweater.  Today we make love
                                  in our minds.
and women come to fore, winning the field.

It is Christmas, Hanukkah,—heritages we leave
                                  behind
            in Israel.

There is a new cross in the wind, and it is our

      minds, imagination, will

      where the discovery is made

of how to pass the night, how to share the gift

of love, our bodies, which is true
                                  illumination
of the present instant.


There is no other journey to make.  We receive all
            we need.
Without insight, we remain blind.
Without vision, we see only this world.

SUPPLICATION: SELECTED POEMS, ed. Joshua Beckman,
C. A. Conrad and Robert Dewhurst, 2015

FRANCES BELLERBY

## A Possible Prayer on New Year's Day

To the Light now invisible
Word now inaudible
Truth now unknowable

Pray for the appearance of shadows
Before this New Year's Night.
For shadow trees on the cold null meadows,
Proof of the sun's light.
And pray for each shadow to be delicate and precise as its tree,
Now and in memory.

*THE FIRST-KNOWN AND OTHER POEMS, 1975*

JEREMY HOOKER

## New Year's Day at Lepe

Set out on a morning of white thaw
smoking between oaks, Hatchet Pond so still
it might have been frozen
except for the long slender rods
as if painted on its dark blue glaze.
Saw nothing of the *Private, Keep Out*
notices of semi-feudal estates,
but cock pheasants in brown fields
of sharp-edged clods, poking out their necks.
Then the small rusty bell of the shingle
tinkled and grated as it dragged,
a shadowy tanker bared its round stern
and Marchwood power station exhaled
a breath which the sun tinged pink;
but of all things none seemed newer
than gravel with its sheen of fresh oranges
at the water's lip.  Brought away that,
and an old transparent moon
over the Island, the delicate industrial sky
blue-grey as a herring gull's back,
and a small sunny boy running beside
the great wet novelty shouting *wasser, wasser.*

THE CUT OF THE LIGHT: POEMS 1965–2005, 2006

ILEANA MALANCIOIU *translated by* MICHAEL LONGLEY

## *Somewhere in Transylvania*

Somewhere in Transylvania in an old church
I saw a saint who carried his skin on his back
But the skin had kept the shape of his body
Just as the saint had held on to his faith.

You could see this from his radiant forehead
And from the raw ribs that didn't seem to hurt
And from the way the skin, his facsimile,
Didn't look in the least light-weight.

Somewhere in Transylvania in an old church
I saw a single body that was prepared to die
He carried his soul on his back in his own skin
As though he was carrying a fortune.

WAVELENGTHS, 2009

PARTAW NADERI *translated by* SARAH MAGUIRE
*and* YAMA YARI

*Relative*


I know the language of the mirror –

its perplexities and mine
spring from one race

our roots can be traced
to the ancient tribe of truth


*Kabul, February 1994*
POEMS, 2008 *in association with the Poetry Translation Centre*

ANNA ADAMS

## Analysis of the Silence

This silence is lack of telephone-bells and traffic,
absence of feet through grass or keels through waves,
the gagging of rumour, or radio-voice and static,

and presence of shrill wren-signals, gannet-dives –
their splash, emergence, wing-claps of self-applause –
and sighs of pale, bottle-glass green sea that heaves

its sandbank mattress over: small motors of bees
that hum low over the ground: furtive crumble of walls,
and secret mitosis of cells in leaves: far cries

of squealing terns, discordant as unoiled wheels
above the deafening roar in the hub of the world's
invisible dynamo thundering here, that feels

like silence.  But here, where deft gannets pin chiffon folds
of water scarves, I can hear, under all, the terrific
engines.  Here is the axle-tree that holds

the planet in place, and controls the unsleeping traffic.

GREEN RESISTANCE: NEW AND SELECTED POEMS, 1996

MARIN SORESCU *translated by* MICHAEL LONGLEY

## The Resurrection of Lazarus

God, what have you done to me,
Just when I was beginning to unwind!

It was like having my eyes demystified
And learning to see in the dark.
From a biochemical point of view
I was looking at a different moon.

It was like unmuffling my eardrums
And receiving the song of myself
Loud and clear on all wavelengths.
I made it up as I went along.

Now I feel I've been out for the count
And am coming round, punchdrunk as usual.
You are the burglar, the grave-robber.
You are the one who mugged me.


WAVELENGTHS, 2009

FRANCES BELLERBY

## The Sunset of that Day

Lazarus dare not raise his eyes
above the hooded valley.
Dare not level his weak sight
with that flooded glory.
Death-black on crystal clarity
a coast line there
edges a wide estuary
of primrose water fair
and smiling as though nothing had to die.
Time displaying eternity.

This peace and loveliness
Lazarus cannot share,
nor that most gentle shadowless
further honey-gold shore
detailed there in light:
rock-bound pools, sand,
shallow coves beneath kind
woods which lie deliberate
as gentle beasts at rest,
sun-yellow in that shadowless
light unseen by Lazarus,
death's brief departed guest.

So there'll be no recall
of this first evening of his resurrection
except by touch of grass
cool to the feet – and quickly then
blackbird's loud rattling call.
It will be this and this

that store for Lazarus all
his dazed and trembling bliss,
his charmed and freshened life
brilliant with death, the ratified
lord of his heart still safe,
still uncrucified.

THE FIRST-KNOWN AND OTHER POEMS, 1975

John Lawrence, *Church and Moon*, illustration from
*Light Unlocked: Christmas Card Poems* (2005)

RUTH PITTER

## Who Knows?

I hope you heard it as well. I thought of you.
Commonsense as the stalking-horse of delusion we always knew,
But it didn't come from the physicists then. Solid matter,
Sensuous evidence we began to be weaned from; now the latter
Has to take a back seat more and more; contradiction
Our daily bread, our spatial references largely fiction,
And I'm glad of it. Mirth and glee are on the run
In our social world, but here they have begun;
These men are beginning to say what he said before.
We can strip off some of the stinking rags we wore,
And under the wicked-stepmother sky gambol like God's lambs.
Someone should say this soon in elegant dithyrambs,
But I haven't time just now. And the other bit,
Anti-matter – did you hear? I cannot get over it;
Those galaxies in the depth could easily be
Something that could dismiss into eternity,
Into pure energy, into pure light and heat
This excellent planet so firm under our feet,
This wonderful flesh and bone, those stars out there,
And leave little trace of them or itself anywhere.
It does remind one. This order must pass, he said.
The circle of thought is closing. Are you afraid?
Since we are his, I hope that you like me
Take this (delightful but wholly unnecessary) corroboration
                                        with mirth and glee.


COLLECTED POEMS, 1990

FRANCES CORNFORD

## Epitaph for Everyman

My heart was more disgraceful, more alone,
And more courageous than the world has known.

O passer-by, my heart was like your own.

SELECTED POEMS, *ed. Jane Dowson, 1996*

KEVIN CROSSLEY-HOLLAND

*The Language of Yes*


This world's wreckers are at their games
and everywhere it is late.

Words words words a fury of words
hype and shred and prate,
sanitise, speculate;
they please themselves.

How can I be content
with hollow professions
or the arm's length of the sceptic?
Even with the sensory,
the pig heart's slop-and-mess?

I still want.

Let me make and remake the word
which reveals itself,
unexpected, always various,

and be so curious
(affirmation's mainspring)
I sing the language of yes.


THE LANGUAGE OF YES, 1996

Cecil Collins, *Tree*, frontispiece to Kathleen Raine's
*Six Dreams and other poems* (1968)

KATHLEEN RAINE

# The Door that Opens on Two Sides*

I do not know when precisely I first began looking for that door—the door that opens from the outer into the inner world, the House of the Soul. There must be many, perhaps most human beings, who never experienced, as I did even in my childhood, the sense of loss and exile, of looking for something else, some other reality that accorded more with my needs and desires, than the world as I found it. But there must be few who have not, since childhood, hoped for, or even only despaired of, some glimpse of the order of supernatural values that alone can explain or justify that relation between the human being and his world.

The past, the future, and the imaginable. These ways of search first occur to us. The imaginable—the world of dreams. The fairy-tale, that opens the door for the Dancing Princesses, beyond which lie the groves of silver trees, the lake, the underground palace, and the beautiful princes. It is the door that in sleep we open, and find beyond it the things we most desire. But it is all illusion, and that we know very well, and wake in tears. In dreams, too, we seek to re-enter the past, our own past. And waking, we beat on the door of memory, to let us in. And all the epics and ballads and chronicles of history are the blood and meal that feed the shades of the past, bringing back Achilles and Hector, Dido and Cressida, and innumerable men and their creations. But like ghosts, they are fixed for ever in their final forms. We cannot change the fate of Julius Caesar, cannot save Hector, or turn Æneas's ship from Carthage, or add a day to the life of Marlowe or of Mary Queen of Scots, or change the outcome of Waterloo in 1815 or the Battle of France in 1940. The past is a prison, where events lie in the rigor of their own death like fossils, gradually sinking lower in the strata of time, losing their contours, and crumbling away into non-existence.

And the future offers no more than the past, though perhaps not entirely inaccessible to crystal-gazers and fortune-tellers. I have riddled it often by turning up the cards, taking sortes from Dryden's Virgil, and

Hafiz, and the Bible. There is, I think, more than coincidence in the frequency with which such forecasts are verified. But there is a shrivelled and ape-like inhumanity about the future of fortune-tellers, the quality of a dead foetus. The walls of time and place do not open to give us freedom, but instead, close in on us, and we have the sense of the world not expanding but shrinking. To read the crabbed prophecies of Nostradamus is to experience that sense of the shrinking of time to a degree that our sensory make-up normally and mercifully spares us. It is to experience the closing in of the burning walls of Poe's story of the Pit and the Pendulum. Crystal-gazing is not that door into the inner world. For that is continually present, and neither past nor future nor fantasy. Perhaps it need not be looked for at all, perhaps one finds it only when one has stopped looking.

One closes the door of an evening, and sitting under the lamp, with the shutters closed, and the world turning outside, making the wind that blows along the top of the fells, and moving the stars in their rigid rotation round the sky. Everything is still in the room—that is, everything is perfectly present. Nothing marks the passage of time. The growth of the hyacinth in the glass, the crumbling of logs into ashes, take place so slowly that they do not disturb the mind. It is at such times that the door opens. The objects in the room do not visibly change. It is as if they step aside, with a sort of rustle that one can almost hear, as if a real curtain were pulled back.

And then, one is in eternity. The things present are there too. Only, the perception of them is different. They are inexplicably holy. One sees beyond them and through them, they are continuous with all that ever preceded or will follow them, and with everything in the world. They imply and extend to the four points of the compass, every place on earth, and every time past or time to come. The spirit, for the time, is free, seeing the chairs, the flowers on the table, the curtains, the lamp and the dust, for what they are, an appearance on the surface of a continuous, living, single universe. The spirit is passionately, consciously, and fully satisfied.

Then, the log drops in the hearth; or the mind stirs, and the curtain closes again, one is back in the dimensions of time and place. The room comes back into place with another inaudible rustle. One tries, for a moment, to force the door again. But it is locked from the inside. There is no choice but to yield to the weariness of mind that follows, and to sleep; or to take up the book that one is reading or writing and set one's mind to work; or to go into the cold kitchen and put the oatmeal to soak in the porridge saucepan, and the kindling to dry in the oven, and lay the breakfast for the next day.

That is the door that lovers too are looking for. Sometimes perhaps they find it and enter together. For sex is an everyday mysticism, and can perhaps be much more. Is there any human being whose heart's desire is not to be, with another loved person, there? I believe that it must be possible. But I know only of the way that one goes alone. And I believe that, after all, the sorrowful and lonely way is easier for most of us, than the dangerous way of happiness. The discipline of joy and beauty is only attained by the rarest and finest of souls. Like the music of Mozart, the painting of Raphael, and the architecture of Greece, the serenity of beauty marks a peak rarely reached in human history or in human life. Tragedy is our commonplace, and suffering is the only school in which most of us ever learn anything. But of all human souls, I most honour those who have submitted themselves to the discipline of beauty and joy, and have not lost their purity of heart in it.

It is not entirely to our credit that we live in a world in which miracles practically cannot happen. For a miracle is an event that reaches a certain quality. We have lost the sense of quality that would know a miracle from a coincidence or an optical illusion. The seeing of visions is an experience entirely qualitative. But most visions raise the world, as it were, only by one power. At most we detect the molecules, so to speak, by their propulsion of larger bodies; or perhaps not even that, but only (to use the simile of the microscope still) the revolutions of the chromosomes and the astral figures; or even, with our poor lenses, only the almost visible cells, that are, nevertheless, enough to shock us with the realisation of further penetration that might be made with better instruments. I can find no better image.

The interior castle, the house of the soul. If by chance we stray into it, without chart or compass, how little we know. And yet, to the saints, it is such a well-charted territory, so thoroughly explored, as familiar as the ordinary appearance of the world to the senses. Not surprisingly, for there is no duality. The supernatural world is the world we ordinarily know and see and walk about in. There is no other. For any rose can be the mystic rose. So seen it is not less a rose, but more a rose.

They are everywhere, the shapes of beauty, contoured on the edges of the mountains, drawn on the walls and pavements of cities by sun and shadow whose shape defines them, draws them. Any object, however poor, will serve for their incarnation. What more is there, then, than the material object itself? In fact, there is nothing more, only we can so see material objects that we no longer recognise them, for they are no longer material in the common sense, but holy, seen in depth. We see not partially, but all of them, their true nature, or rather a little more of that nature, raised to a higher power, to use again the simile of science, beyond which the thing seen extends yet further into a brightness that remains dark to us.

As I write, the guns are firing over London, and the night is torn. The world's material texture is so flimsy—strange that our bodies still instinctively believe that it is so solid. Our whole life is like walking on the water—we do not sink, light waves bear us up and are our terra firma. Yet, in an instant, they could stop, and then the world would vanish. It is so fragile; and all this night, fire and explosions and hurtling pieces of iron are tearing holes in it. A storm shaking the solid data of our conviction, the conviction innate in our animal bodies, that the earth is solid underfoot.

*FACES OF DAY AND NIGHT, 1972*

EDMUND WHITE

# from *Record Time*

I'd come home from school by way of the library, my biceps aching from
my burden of records, scores and books, and I'd barricade myself in my
room. As the Chicago night began to fall earlier and earlier each December
evening and the snow on my sill would melt and refreeze, I took comfort
in my room with the sizzling radiator, the chocolate brown walls, tan
burlap curtains, gleaming maple chest of drawers, comfortable arm chair
and the old brass lamp from my earliest childhood, originally designed
before my time as a gas lamp but now rewired with its glass chimney still
intact and its luminosity still capable of being dialled down into yellow
dimness. I loved the coarse red wool blanket with its big Hudson Bay dull
satin label sewn into the upper left-hand corner like a commemorative
stamp showing a moose and a canoe. I loved the pale celadon green
pots I'd bought in Chinatown, their raised designs nearly effaced under
heavy glazes, their wide cork tops sealed shut with red wax that had to
be chipped away to reveal the candied ginger slices within, floating, slimy,
in a thick, dark sugar syrup. Now the ginger had long since been eaten
and the bowls washed clean but they were still faintly redolent of their
spicy, mysterious original contents. I loved my seven bronze Chinese
horses, which were stored in a brown velvet box cut into exact silhouettes
into which the little statues could be wedged. Each horse was different,
head lowered in a gentle arc to graze or thrown back to gallop, each
weighty and cold in the hand. I loved my music boxes given to me one
by one, Christmas after Christmas: the turning brass cylinder under glass
plucking brass tines that played the Gounod waltz from *Faust*; the
unpainted wood Swiss chalet with the mirrors for windows that played
'Edelweiss'; the miniature grand piano; the revolving water mill. But I was
less impressed by the look of each box than by the richness of its sound.
The Gounod I liked the best since the sound wasn't tinny but resonant
and the box, if I held it, throbbed in my hand with expensive precision.

I loved the smell of the boxes of tea I collected and scarcely ever drank

– I'd inhale the dry, smoky perfume of the lapsang souchong leaves, the Christmassy clove and orange odor of the Constant Comment, the acrid smell of Japanese gunpowder green tea, not really like a tea at all but a kind of grass, or so I imagined. I loved the way the hard metal lids fit snugly into these square boxes and had to be pried open with the handle of a spoon. I loved sitting on the floor, my back propped against the bed as I turned the broad, smooth pages of the opera scores in which the original words were translated, very approximately, into the same number of English syllables so that one could sing along. I'd keep changing the stacks of 78s, some of them so badly gouged that I'd have to nudge the needle out of a deep crevasse, others so worn down that my needle, itself not ideally sharp, would just slide over the bald surface in a split-second condensation of long minutes' worth of music.

RECORD TIME, 2002

DAVID HOCKNEY

# from *My Yorkshire**

*(an interview with Marco Livingstone in Hockney's Bridlington studio, 2010)*

. . . Lots of people don't see pictures as just an account of seeing. They think that's what the thing itself is. A lot will blow up soon: financial, political, artistic, perhaps, which I think might be rather good. Because right at the moment you've got an art world that is just being very corrupted by the money, and the only thing now about art is that it's worth a lot of money. That's all it does.

How many artists look at the world? They seem to think, 'Oh, we know what the world looks like now, why bother? Let's go inside, this, that and the other.' Well, that's the great thing. We don't really know what it looks like. It's too complicated.

I have realized, when we go out, that we have our own little places now. They are all near here. We don't go down near Warter any more. The motifs are all within 20 minutes of this house. The farthest away is the 'tunnel', about 20 or 25 minutes away. But loads of the motifs I return to are just ten minutes away, so it's easy to go look. And as we kept looking over the years, I've come to understand that there's so much to see that you edit in your head. That's how we look. There's more colour there than you think, far more, but you have to look.

Looking is a positive act. It's good to deliberately look. People only go deliberately to look when they go in the Louvre: they are looking at pictures, tourists, generally. They look at a building, they look at the Grand Canyon. Van Gogh told you this: that just immediately around you, it's always interesting. I'm looking at you here in your suit, with this torn fabric on the chair. Or Maurice Payne, with his old face and his 'young' leather jacket. Even if you never left this room, there would be enough subjects, especially with the occasional person coming in.

*MY YORKSHIRE, 2011*

David Hockney, *Summer Road Near Kilham* (2008), inkjet-printed computer drawing
reproduced in *My Yorkshire* (2011)

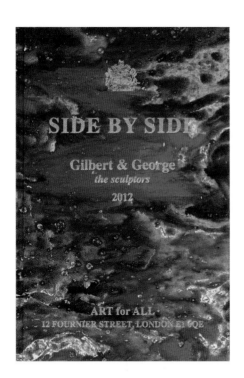
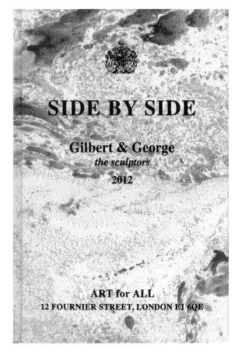
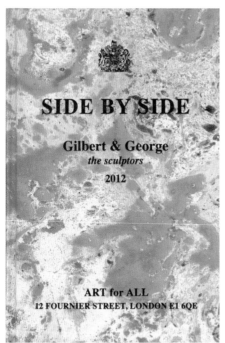
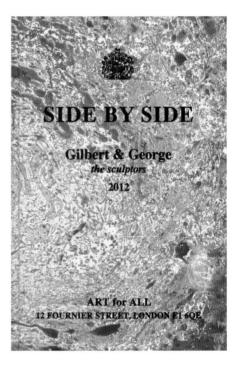

Linen covers for *Side by Side* (2012), hand-marbled by Gilbert & George

Peter Blake, *The Sailors' Arms*, original print from
the *de luxe* edition of *Under Milk Wood* (2014)

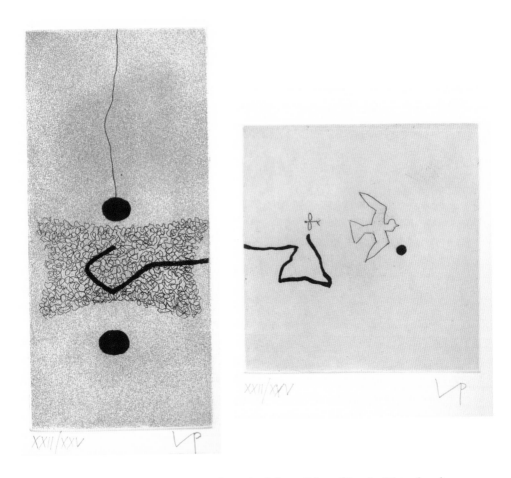

Victor Pasmore, two etchings from the *de luxe* edition of *Burning Waters* (1995)

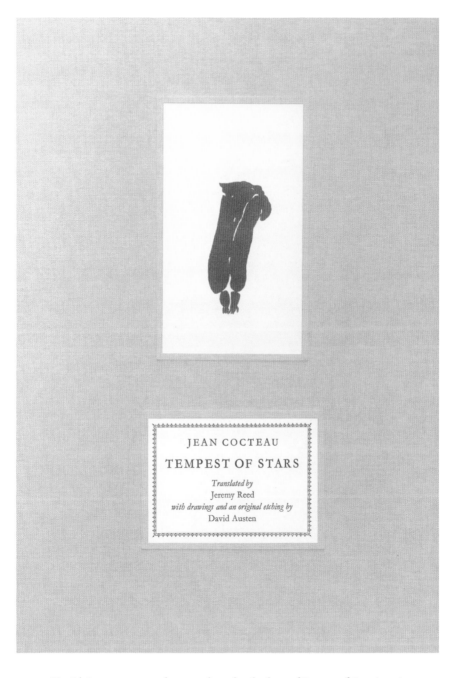

David Austen, watercolour on the solander box of *Tempest of Stars* (1992)

Jim Dine, *Head of Homer*, etching from the *de luxe* edition of
Neil Curry's *The Bending of the Bow* (1993)

Paula Rego, *Girl Reading at Window*, lithograph reproduced in *Jane Eyre* (2003)
Paula Rego, *Death Goes Shopping*, etching from the *de luxe* edition of *I Have Found a Song* (2010)

28/75                     Kitaj

R. B. Kitaj, *Anne Atik*, lithograph from the *de luxe* edition of *Offshore* (1991)

JAMES FENTON

# Going to See Michael and Edna

I was in the front room of my home in the Conway Valley, poking the coal fire one afternoon, when a great SWOOSH-BANG made me say to myself: That sounded like incoming. A second later I had corrected the thought. I was at home, not at war, but the world still sounded like the front line. Every noise had to be analysed. The slamming of doors on Southern Region trains, I remember, still made me alert in those days, like artillery. Waterloo really did sound to me like a battlefield.

I returned to my familiar desk in the window. A field away from the white-rendered farmhouse on the opposite side of the valley rose a column of black smoke. Very soon, helicopters arrived from Valley airbase to investigate. For the noise I had heard was the crashing of a supersonic jet fighter. The crew had ejected less than a thought before, landing on the same startled farm as their annihilated plane.

*     *     *

Michael had invited me to Belfast, and I crossed by the night ferry, arriving at dawn with two heavy cases (I was on my way, ultimately, to a new life in London). I thought: I can't phone Michael and Edna yet – I'll go to the Europa Hotel, eat breakfast and see if I can have a wash and a bit of a rest. When I told the driver of the communal taxi where I was going, he seemed to react with some hostility. But the Europa was the journalists' hotel, so that was not surprising.

And Belfast was a famously hostile place in those days. American reporters in Indochina, hard-bitten guys in safari suits, used to say they had found it by far the scariest place to work in. To be clear, I ought to say that one lurched between extremes of hostility and hospitality. Many people would have been happier to be hospitable, but circumstances had made them hostile.

'Europa Hotel!' sneered the taxi driver in due course. I heaved my bags out and paid, before trudging up what I remember as a sort of ramp that led to the entrance. Only at the last moment did I raise my eyes from the pavement to take in the Europa Hotel. It had been bombed the night before (it was always being bombed) and the ground floor had been devastated. I was like a man checking in to a ruin.

*     *     *

My suitcases were very old, but not very beautiful. They were heavy even when empty. They belonged to the age of porters. One of them had a system of ratcheted levers instead of plain hinges, which encouraged me to overfill the case with books, close it and then sit on it to compact the contents. This made for astonishingly heavy luggage.

I set out across the empty city of Belfast in search of a breakfast, stopping frequently to recover my strength. Nobody, one would have thought, could have mistaken me for a bomber. And yet I remember an agonised look on the face of the café-owner, as I struggled in with my suitcases.

The dawn seemed to be dragging its feet. I remember a large civic square, with subterranean toilets. Someone had driven a Mini in such a way as to up-end it on the steps down to the Gents. It was hard to see how this had been achieved – a feat of jumping over the railings – but there it was.

At around eight o'clock I phoned Michael and Edna. This was early for them, of course, but it was late for me. It was a desolate morning. How grateful I was to Michael when he picked me up. How grateful I am still!

*     *     *

We were due, Michael and I, to take a spin through Donegal. But before we did that, Michael, who was working for the Arts Council of Northern Ireland in those days, had to see a woman at some kind of community centre in Andersonstown or some other Provo-dominated district. Michael comes of Protestant stock, as could be deduced from his name. He is the opposite of a bigot, and has always made himself amiable, and on this occasion he introduced me as a visiting poet from England.

The woman looked at me for a moment. Then she said: 'If your friend is a visiting poet from England, perhaps he'd like to recite one of his poems for us.'

I remember the look that Michael gave me. It said briefly: oh dear, please cooperate, otherwise she might turn nasty.

But he didn't have to warn me. I had immediately picked up the unpleasant implication of her request, and I had already once been held by the IRA on suspicion of being a spy. I had been in serious trouble. But I was thinking: It can't just be any poem, it must be something that sounds to *her* like a poem, and it mustn't be nonsense or flippant either.

I chose to recite a couple of stanzas I had written not long before, describing a morning scene in Battambang, in Cambodia. They were the lines on which an ill-fated longer poem had ground to a halt. I didn't know what to do with them. I don't say they were good – but they addressed the war that was forever on my mind. Indeed I think I was working on those lines when the fighter jet, out of the blue, crashed into the farm opposite my house in Wales. At all events, they were fresh in my mind. When I finished, the woman looked just a little abashed, or so I fancied. And Michael made an appreciative noise, as he sometimes does at the end of a reading.

Often since then I have suggested to aspiring poets that they make sure they write something (even if it is only one thing) that they can read, or recite, with an audience in mind. I say this because people often assume, or are told by their betters, that they are writing for the page. I say: do yourself a favour, write yourself something you can perform. I don't normally say this, however, envisaging that such a poem may help you escape from a tight spot, such as a suspicion of espionage. But there's another of 'the uses of literacy'.

We had a great spin through Donegal, and, as I say, I am always grateful to Michael. Rescue me, Michael, rescue me from this scrape.

*LOVE POET, CARPENTER: MICHAEL LONGLEY AT SEVENTY,*
ed. Robin Robertson, 2009

DAVID GASCOYNE

# from *A Kind of Declaration*[*]

[This is an imaginary interviewer (I.I.) interviewing David Gascoyne.]

*I.I.  What would you as an Englishman like to say to those attending an international gathering of poets?*
D.G.  Above all I should like to quote from one of Wordsworth's sonnets on National Independence and Liberty (1803):

> We must be free or die
> Who speak the tongue which Shakespeare spake . . .

and I would then say that I hope that today this might well be declared by fellow poets throughout the world if transposed in the form of 'who speak the tongue that Dante spake, that Lorca spake, that Camoens spake, that Villon spake, that Pushkin and Blok spake, that Hölderlin spake, that Parmenides and Seferis spake', and so on.

(I must interrupt myself at this point just to add that if I had completed the quotation, it might have tempted me into a completely irrelevant digression concerning faith and morals ('those which Milton held' in Wordsworth's words), an engrossing topic involving Poetry and Revolution (the English and Puritan one to begin with) as well as religious and ethical problems and their relation to this particular preoccupation of mine; but I must leave further consideration of such a possibility for some quite different occasion.)

*I.I.  Do you believe that the poet should be politically committed and that this should influence his writing?*
D.G.  While still in my 'teens I was a Communist. I have read a good deal of Hegel, Marx and Engels, and would still describe myself as a convinced and unrepentant socialist, but it would strike me as tactless to try to introduce a discussion of political principles on an occasion of this kind.

*I.I. Then you do not believe that poetry can be expected to serve as a sort of propaganda?*

D.G. Certainly not. But on the other hand, I decidedly believe that all poetry of any significance does and should provide propaganda of a certain kind.

*I.I. Kindly elucidate.*

D.G. The poetry I refer to as being of true significance is not simply that which is authentic. As Peter Levi has observed, 'in minor modern poetry the experience may be genuine yet the language is not, and it is nothing but authentic language that can express reality in a poem'. The kind of poetry I am thinking of is that which is capable of arousing in the reader that sense of astonishment and wonder at being alive and at the mysterious multiplicity of reality such as has been believed by many thinkers to be the beginning of all true philosophy; and it is in favour of such an experience of wonder that the poetry I mean may be described as constituting a kind of propaganda.

*I.I. Is one to suppose that poetry and philosophy are very closely interrelated in your mind?*

D.G. Indeed they are, and if what I have called significant poetry has content, as of course it is bound to have, then whether the subject be everyday life, the inner life, people or places, the greatness or beastliness of men or the beauty or industrial degradation of Nature, whatever in fact the subject, and there is one to be found I believe in even the best 'Surrealist' poem, then the poem's content will almost certainly prove to be capable of philosophical interpretation, as Heidegger has to my mind conclusively demonstrated in his Hölderlin commentaries and in 'On the Road to Language'; though I should never wish to appear dogmatic about any particular interpretation of any given text. In fact it might be said that the importance of a poem may on one level be gauged by the number of possible interpretations to which it is liable to give rise.

*I.I. Does not philosophical poetry tend to lead the poet into too great a use of abstraction and to an elitist abstruseness?*

D.G. There are two distinct questions to be elucidated here, and I have not the time or space to deal adequately with either. Firstly, as I said somewhat baldly in a recent poem, 'Whales and Dolphins': 'A poem should avoid abstraction and / all forms of private declaration of belief'. One of the most important realizations of modern poets in nearly all the countries about whose poetry I know anything at all has been that one must convey whatever content one has to express (and without more than merely ephemeral content, poetry is hardly worth the trouble it takes to write it, though it may give a certain temporary pleasure to both writer and a superficial type of reader) in as concrete and freshly vivid a way as one is capable of finding. The present condition of all language, overtly poetic or otherwise, is critical, as one would expect in a world-situation of ever-increasing extremity. The avoidance of cliché and inauthentic, unspontaneous diction is a challenge that must be faced every time pen is put to paper. Abstruseness is certainly to be avoided as far as possible, and only a poet positively determined to be labelled cerebral could possibly think of it as an infallible indication of poetic excellence. On the other hand, difficulty in understanding a poem is often something that has to be wrestled with, and the resultant increase of insight in the reader, both into the 'meaning' of the poem and into himself, may prove to be ample compensation to him for his effort. Something of the same sort might incidentally be said in passing about the supposed difficulty of some of the most rewarding and therefore important modern music: once one has familiarized oneself with frequently extreme dissonance and other of the more recent musical innovations, one will surely find one's capacity to appreciate and enjoy music greatly extended. To revert to poetry, were you to enquire what I myself would now try most to aim at achieving supposing I should be able to look forward to producing a handful of new poems to add to those of mine that have already been published, I should answer, I think, concision, terseness, immediacy and 'newness' (never mere novelty). At my age, I doubt very much whether I shall ever be able to achieve this, judging from the poem I referred to just now, which happens to be a 72-line effort produced in response to a request for a contribution to an anthology in aid of the Greenpeace Foundation, and it is ostensibly concerned with Whales and Dolphins, while managing also to contain about half-a-dozen quotations (including one from Kathleen Raine). An interviewee should never lose the opportunity for a little self-advertisement . . .

Should you now wish to lead me back to an attempt to make a purely personal statement about poetry, as apart from the kind of generalizations which are apt to sound glib, I think I ought to begin by saying that ever since 'coming-of-age' at least, and I'm not at all sure when exactly this was, I have been preoccupied in one way or another with the apparent conflict between a concern for Truth, regarded as something ever to be sought for in this life but which one can never be certain of having found without the gift of that ultimate faith for which, if one is granted its achievement, Truth is a Person, and the pursuit of poetry, which Pascal, for instance, regarded as a probably frivolous diversion from what should be our most constant and overriding concern. One cannot know what Pascal would have made of the suggestion of George Herbert (admittedly no Jansenist) that:

A verse may find him who a sermon flies,
And turn delight into a sacrifice.

At the same time, the aphoristic form, of which Pascal is surely one of the great masters (by accident, as it happens, since the *Pensées* are no more than notes for a lengthy treatise), may be regarded as being very closely related to that of poetic expression, if one accepts as one of poetry's many possible definitions that it is the distillation of essences. Certainly other outstanding aphorists have been poets, Lao Tsu, Novalis, Coleridge, Blake, Baudelaire, and Nietzsche (the latter more a philosopher than a poet, but who did write some, I understand, not inconsiderable poetry) to name but a few. Poetry and Truth, then, may be seen as contradictory concerns. Pilate's question may have always seemed like a jest, but to me it is rather a philosophical one. (Nowadays it is thought rather funny to ask 'What is Man?') We are familiar with Keats' answer to the question: I have always found it highly questionable. Christianity is quite as disturbing as it may be consoling. Truth is undeniably sometimes hideous, as the suffering not only of Christ but of innumerable ordinary human beings, not to speak of children and animals, about whose sufferings we have only recently begun to be adequately aware, should make obvious.

It may be safely assumed that I do not 'believe in' astrology; but being a Libran, I am undoubtedly given to weighing up the pros and cons; so I will once more say here that 'at the same time' Heidegger, not my principal *maître à penser*, though I have already referred to him, seems to me to be at least partially right in asserting that the essence of Truth is freedom. And I believe that although we are always declaring our love of it and professing our willingness to die in defence of it, as to which I said at the outset that I hoped modern poets of all countries would agree with Wordsworth's sentiments as expressed in a famous sonnet, I also happen to believe that the majority of us are *frightened* of freedom and employ an enormous amount of ingenuity in avoiding, by means of verbal camouflage, casuistry and a variety of other forms of self-deception, ever having to exercise the free will we are always arguing about and which I believe we do indeed possess.

Here again I find myself in danger of being led away into too long a digression, this time on the subject of fear. It is certainly a key-word in any sort of analysis of the contemporary situation, and above all in existential thought about it. The distinction has been drawn, first by Kierkegaard and then by Heidegger, each in his own different way, between dread, fear and anxiety. That this is the Age of Anxiety has by now for long already become a cliché of the kind I observed earlier one has to keep trying to avoid. But that fear is a predominant factor in the condition of the modern psyche is an inescapable fact. Fear of what? It is difficult to draw up any list of a precise length, or to name the fears we are prone to in order of pre-eminence or intensity, but if I might be permitted to make reference to something written some time ago by myself, in *Night Thoughts* I referred to the fear of fear itself, of failure, of uncertainty and loss, of change, of strangeness and strangers, fear of Love, which is perhaps the most basic and which sometimes adopts complicated forms of which at least one is familiar to most of us, and 'the exhausting fear of Death and Mystery'. I might well have included the fear of being oneself, of recognizing and accepting in oneself the capacity for cruelty, destructiveness and violence; but I concluded my catalogue in that particular passage with fear of

Nothing, absolutely Nothing. In this I was no doubt influenced by Heidegger's 'What is Metaphysics?', which I first read in Henry Corbin's pioneer French translation before the War and which made a deep impression on me. 'Nothing – how can it be for science anything other than a horror and a phantasm?' asks Heidegger. But, as he goes on to demonstrate later in the lecture, it is not merely science and scientists who have such a horror of Nothing that they will not allow it to be alluded to, but it is something of which everyone may be supposed to have some sort of experience, specifically in a rarely encountered but ultimately unavoidable form of boredom, that now universal malady of industrialized man. At this point Heidegger draws the distinction already referred to between fear and 'dread'. 'Dread differs absolutely from fear . . . We are always afraid of this or that definite thing . . .' Obviously I cannot give a detailed summary of the lecture here, but will conclude by saying that the essential point to be made is that in a peculiar state of boredom, we have an 'uncanny' feeling of indifference and of the withdrawal of 'what-is-in-totality', which leaves us with nothing to hold on to but nothingness. 'Dread reveals Nothing'. And the philosopher significantly concludes in his Postscript that it is those who are most courageous who are the readiest to undergo the experience of dread in which is revealed the Nothing which, according to him, is the basis of all Metaphysics, a domain in which ordinary logic has to be 'suspended', and in fact altogether abandoned.

Believers are told that the fear of God is the beginning of Wisdom. Those who are still brave enough to call themselves Christians believe in a God they have been brought up to address as our Father. A loving Father is not terrifying. There is puzzle and paradox in all this, and a kind of declaration concerning poetry is not the place to enter into a theological discussion. But what I have been trying to lead up to is some expression of what, in my belief, constitutes perhaps the most important function of poetry in the world at present, and here theology of *some* kind is highly relevant. I believe that it is for poets first and foremost to testify to the existence of something the lack of which, all the evidence today would seem to show, is everywhere beginning to be felt and recognized, and that is, to employ *faute de mieux* one more already hackneyed and inadequate expression, the dimension of the Transcendent. And as one might expect of a critical historical situation, it is, thank heavens, actually producing in poetry a response which shows an awareness of this lack and of the need to express the general longing for a way to fill it. Two lines from the last stanza of a poem by Dannie Abse, who is a full-time doctor and a 'sceptical' humanist as well as a poet, strike me as typical of the kind of feeling that haunts more and more poets who do not feel they have been gifted with the grace of faith in anything more than mortal humanity:

> There are moments when a man must sing
> of a lone Presence he cannot see.
> . . . . . .
> There are moments when a man must praise
> the astonishment of being alive,
> when small mirrors of reality blaze
> into miracles; and there's One always
> who, by never departing, almost arrives.

[*the interview continues*]


SELECTED PROSE 1934–1996, *ed. Roger Scott, 1998*

DANNIE ABSE

## More than a Green Placebo

At an animated dinner party, our host told us how a certain doctor, on
investigating the verbal composition of articles published in the *British
Medical Journal*, had discovered that, on average, 42% of the words in each
issue were adjectives. After some further discussion, I asked, 'Is it worth
travelling around the world to count the cats of Zanzibar?' Satisfied that
I had triumphantly put all opposing discourse to an end with that propi-
tious quotation from Thoreau, I sat back, smugly, waiting for the pudding
to be served.

Then, unexpectedly, one of the guests, John Heath-Stubbs, emphati-
cally replied, 'Yes!' He provoked laughter because of his intervention, and
urgently he repeated, 'Yes, yes, it *is* worth going around the world to count
the cats of Zanzibar.'

John Heath-Stubbs, besides being a poet, is a considerable scholar; and
at that time I thought it was as a scholar that he had answered Thoreau's
rhetorical question in the affirmative. After all, scholars, like scientists,
should not prejudge the value of any harmless investigation before it is
embarked upon. But I suspect others at that dinner table believed that
Heath-Stubbs replied 'Yes' because he was a poet.

Most people, after all, have as little regard for the activity of writing
poems as they have for the kind of scholarship that involves the counting
of adjectives in successive issues of the *BMJ*. They are somewhat baffled
by those who are engaged in such apparently useless activity, unless that
activity brings monetary reward or is simply an expression of a hobby.
Writing poetry as a central concern, not as a marginal pastime, year in
year out, putting the right words in the right order for no evident reason,
neither wishing to persuade anybody nor to legislate, must seem to many
a very odd occupation indeed. No wonder I'm asked, as no doubt other
poets are, 'Do you really consider writing poetry important?' They are
politely asking, 'Why is a grown man like you playing with words?'

In an attempt to justify one's trade as a poet, it is no longer possible to resort to arguing the moral nature of poetry. Those nineteenth-century claims that 'Poetry strengthens the faculty which is the organ of the moral nature of man in the same manner as exercise strengthens a limb' (*A Defence of Poetry*, P. B. Shelley) seem hollow now post-Auschwitz and Hiroshima. Even T. S. Eliot's 'poetry refines the dialect of the tribe' seems in all its ambiguities to be a grandiose assertion, if not a dubious one. The very multiplicity of definitions about the function of poetry proves, does it not, that most people are suspicious that poetry has no function? I know of no long essays in defence of carpentry or in defence of surgery. Everyone is convinced that carpenters and surgeons are necessary. Even so, if by chance professional poets somehow commanded, in the future, regular salaries, I suspect there would be fewer essays in defence of poetry; and if that salary were substantial, no longer would poets be thought of as playing childish word-games, a sort of Radio Three Scrabble.

However, poetry does have several uses. For instance, lately I have been reading an interesting, vulnerable, often touching anthology of verses that have been written out of, or about, mental disorder. The anthology is called *Beyond Bedlam* and originated with a group at the Maudsley Hospital, London, who had asked, among other questions, what role can poetry have in alleviating symptoms of mental distress? One knows that patients can be consoled by reading poetry, and many doctors have no doubt seen, as I have, a volume of poems at the bedside of a terminally ill patient. But what the editors of *Beyond Bedlam* were interested in was how the act of writing poetry by patients themselves can be beneficial.

In 1973–74, I was privileged to be writer-in-residence at Princeton University. One of my duties for that American academic year was to preside over a small class of aspiring student-writers. Each week they presented me with their new-minted poems, most in foetal condition, and these were discussed, closely examined, winked at, criticised, and not entirely dismissed, for as Johnson once pithily remarked, 'The price of reading other people's poetry is praise.'

I did feel sometimes that these weekly sessions seemed more to resemble group therapy than the routine enterprise of a literary work-shop. One of the students, an anxious, very bright, young woman had been having periodic weekend migraine attacks, but these almost always failed to keep their appointments during that academic year. Was it a coincidence? One day, she laughingly remarked, 'Reading and writing poetry is a green placebo, Dr Abse.'

I was interested that she had defined poetry as such. A 1972 editorial in *The Lancet* referred to the power of placebos: 'Although it is more satisfying to the practitioner to ascribe a favourable response to his wise choice of pharmacological agent, it is sadly true that up to three-quarters of patients with affective disorders improve with placebo alone.' That hardly surprising assertion went on to discuss, among other matters, less well-known facts such as the importance of tablet colour in the prescribing of a placebo. Though depression responded most favourably to yellow tablets, the green ones worked their magic with greater proficiency in treating anxiety than either those coloured yellow or red.

Of course, poetry is more than a green placebo because, apart from any questionable therapeutic use, it can metastasise in major and minor ways. W. H. Auden was defeatist when he cried out: '. . . poetry makes nothing happen: it survives / In the valley of its making where executives / Would never want to tamper'. He wrote those lines under a benign government.

Once poets sat at the Prince's right hand and praised the Prince. Their lies, if beautiful enough, may have contributed to the myth-making of history. Now poets, especially those who live in authoritarian societies, no longer sit at the Prince's right hand but, like others, may suffer the decisions of that powerful figure and are almost obligated to bear witness as best they can. Writing out of their own personal predicament, they may affect others who share that predicament or who are in sympathy with that predicament. No one can measure the small detonations of poems that have in their own idioplasm a sociohistorical implication. Poems can become, according to social circumstances, subversive documents.

THE TWO ROADS TAKEN, 2003

## FRANCES BELLERBY

# Come to an End

In the afternoon of that shining day suddenly there was no more to be done by Stella and the doctor. So the doctor went away, and Hugh and Stella stood together without seeing each other outside the closed door of Jill's room. He said: 'I think I'll go and meet Simon's bus.' And she answered from somewhere distant: 'Yes, that's the best plan, and it must be near his time now.' Then, again as often during his hours of waiting that day, Hugh was reminded of Jill's birth eight years ago, when Stella had nearly died; when at last he had been allowed to go to her he had not known how to speak because of the great distance between them. He had gone from her to Simon, who was three and a half, and told him about his young sister; and Simon had listened, his face very red, staring at the ground.

Hugh walked across the fields to meet Simon's bus bringing him back from school.

The sky was radiantly blue. The hedges were tawny, orange, crimson. There was no wind. The warmth, stillness, sword-brightness had for Hugh the quality of a dream – a quality not of Time but of Eternity. And as he walked he was aware, without surprise, resentment, or any definite emotion, that his whole life had led him, by quite obvious though subtly chosen paths, to this 'place', this 'time', that were outside Space and Time. For he had come to an end: from here no path led away, for there was nothing beyond; to have reached this afternoon was the purpose of his existence – an infinitesimal scrap of the Purpose of all Life.

All he had to do now was to meet Simon's bus. Was that all? Well, he'd have to say something, to tell Simon something—And he hadn't told it to himself yet, he hadn't yet put it into words in his own mind—But with every step across the sun-flooded fields he drew nearer to Simon. Oh, he must think, think! The right words existed, even for this – he must find them.

Only, thought of such a kind proved impossible. As he stood – waiting again – under the chestnut tree outside the inn he could think of nothing but the number of glossily shining chestnuts amongst the fallen leaves in which Simon and Jill would have been interested.

Then he noticed Mrs Pring, the innkeeper's wife, peering through her lace half-curtains, her huge red face eager with grief and curiosity. For a moment he wondered what was the matter with her, till he remembered, as though it had been far in the past, that Jill had been brought back along this bit of road in the morning by the doctor and the people in the car. Oh, then Mrs Pring, the whole village, would know about it – would know everything except what he had come to tell Simon. Before long they'd know that also – trust them.

Distraught, feeling his dream-like certainty ebb before the frightful isolation caused by the sight of Mrs Pring's peering, he laid his hand for support on the old wall near him. Immediately he forgot Mrs Pring. For he became aware of the stone wall, wondered who had built it, what manner of man, to what accompaniment of thought, in what weathers. And in a clear flash it was evident to him that the builder of the wall was also in this thing. Why? Possibly the making of the wall had been *his* purpose, his end of existence. Be that as it might, touching the cool stone of the other man's wall was like touching the spirit of the other man's hand; and that, to Hugh in his present state, was unspeakable beneficence.

Simon's bus came swinging round the corner.

Besides small Simon there were in it several large women with vast shopping-bags. Suddenly the idea struck Hugh that these women would have heard of Jill's accident, and would somehow, with their soft-hearted, pushing pachydermosity, have managed to be the first to 'break the sad news'. Raging with anger and anxiety he strolled forward, greeting each of them pleasantly, nonchalantly, holding them far away so that no one, not even horse-faced Mrs Hodges, could dare to speak to him. They all climbed down and vanished. Then came Simon, grinning slightly, saying: 'Hullo, Dad.'

Speak, speak, speak, cried Hugh to himself. 'Good day, son?' he asked. This had been his usual greeting, he remembered, but fool that he was to use it now.

'Not bad.' Simon kicked a stone, jumped an ant-heap with his feet together, stooped to choose a grass-stalk. He wouldn't look up. That meant he was deeply moved.

'I say, Simon—' but Hugh broke off, startled at the extraordinarily high pitch of his voice.

Simon climbed on a white gate they were passing. Keeping his back turned he took his feet off the bar and poised on his hands, very straight, head up, saying casually: 'I've got them all right, Dad.'

'Got them?' Hugh's mind jerked violently.

'Um. Mr Bailey said it was the first time but one that any chap in his Form had got House Football Seconds. He said Montague was the other – he became Captain of the School. He seemed quite bucked. I say, let's get on home – I've a beastly lot of prep.—' He jumped away from the gate to the ground. Hugh felt his impatience to be home and telling Stella and Jill this incomparable news. He'd tell it casually, appearing pre-occupied with something else, flaming with excitement.

Hugh leant heavily on the white gate. He began to speak. When he stopped he couldn't recall what he had said. He was almost sure he hadn't told Simon that Jill was dead, but someone else had. Had they? Who? The man whose hand he'd touched when he'd laid his hand on the wall?

He looked round. Simon stood with his head bent over a bit of stick he was peeling. He'd dropped his books. His face was crimson, his lower lip caught between his teeth.

The sun's rays would soon be nearly level across the quiet fields. But it was clear to Hugh that, though night came, though another day, with fresh light, dawned, though this summer would soon be forgotten, and then autumn, winter, and spring, though years and years would pass, and Simon might live to a great age and then be forgotten also, yet this moment would not ever pass. Here he stood, and here stood Simon, in eternity. Thither all their paths had led, but there was no path hence for either of them.

SELECTED STORIES, 1986

EDWARD THOMAS

# Milking

The end of April was sappy, careless, and profuse. One day it was all eagerness and energy and gave no rest to the wind and the sun, on the earth or in the waters or in the clouds of the sky, and the songs of the birds were a mad medley. Another day it was indolent: a soft grey sky without form covered all; there was no wind; the birds were still; the lusty, buxom spring, a pretty and merry slut, with her sleeves and skirts tucked up and her hair down over her eyes and shoulders, had fallen asleep in the midst of her toil and nothing could waken her but a thunderstorm in the night. The next day she was simply at play with showers and sunlight, sunlight and showers, at play with sky and earth as if they were but coloured silks and now she fluttered the white and blue and green together and then, wearying of that, held up the grey and the grey-white and the green, and lastly mingled all together inextricably. For the most part she preferred not to let either go quite out of sight; when the heavy rain fell on the rustling wood it was out of a sky serene, lustrous, and mild; and when the light was steady and the rain tripping away from it upon myriad feet down among the leaves to the earth, still the shadows of the rain clouds stole over the hills like smoke. There was a gamesome spirit abroad. It was seen in the amorous conflict of rain and sun, and heard in the cry of the titmouse along the hedge: 'Fitchy! fitchy!'

Rain or not, always far away in the south there was a cluster of white peaks apparently belonging to a land that knew neither our sun nor our rain. Rain or sunshine or both made little difference to the shed at the cross roads. It was shadowy and old under a roof that was patched and hollowed like the sail of a ship. The door was open, but on either side the piles of dung were high and long and allowed the sun to enter the shed only for half an hour each day. And now in that half-hour the farmer Weekes was going to milk the last of his seven cows. Until now he had known of the afternoon only that the wind whined in the roof and that the rain dripped through on to his back at intervals. When the sun at last stepped in between the banks of dung he could see that it was a forward spring. For his eye travelled up between the green walls of the road to the hills four miles away, and there the beech trees were almost in perfect leaf and in their dense ranks resembled a flock of sheep with golden fleeces descending the slope. Yet it wanted a week before May-day. The grass was good, and already the cows were clean and bright after their winter in the yard; and, having looked at his hands alongside the white and strawberry hide of the cow, he got up and wiped them on a wisp of grass beside the door. He stood there a moment – a tall, crooked man, with ever-sparkling eyes in a nubbly and bony head, worn down by sun and toil and calamity to nothing but a stone, hollowed and grey, to which his short black hair clung like moss; in his starved fields you might have found a weathered flint of the same shape, and have said that it was much like a man's head. He stretched himself, and then turned and called the cow by her name in a voice so deep and powerful that it was as if the whole shed and not a man's chest had uttered it.

He sat down again to milk and to think, with his face turned to the sun. He was thinking of the farmhouse under those woods on the hill, where he used to go courting twenty years ago, and of the girl, the only daughter of that house, who was now his wife. He had driven over there one day in his father's cart to see about some pigs. The old man had given him supper, honey and bread and butter, cold apple dumplings with cheese, and cowslip wine. It was a wonderful quiet house, very dark under tall beeches, with a quality in the dark still air as if it were under water, but very clean and bright with china and brass and the white tablecloth and the old man's white beard and glittering blue eyes. He knew that the old man was failing to make both ends meet, but there was no sign of it, and he spoke with a cheerful gravity, and there was a look about house and man as if they were apart from the world, and not subject to such accidents as failure of crops, cattle disease, and the like. They had done their business, and at the end of a long silence he was thinking of rising to go, when Emily, the daughter, came in without noticing him, kissed her father, and said, 'Father, there is a white bird in the old apple tree of the rickyard singing like a blackbird. Yet 'tis as white as milk.'

'Well, we will all come and see,' said the old man, and then she saw that a stranger was there, and with a blush she retreated and opened the door. As she was shutting it she turned round out of curiosity, thus revealing her own face to the stranger, but seeing nothing of his which was in shadow. In a minute or two they went out into the rickyard where the cart was waiting. Emily was patting the horse's neck, but with her face towards the old apple tree where a white blackbird was singing from the topmost branch. 'You will not let them shoot it, father, will you?' she said. The white bird and its song, the girl's fair hair, and rosy face very serious, the unbent old man soon to die, the sombre smouldering old tiles and brick wall of the house, and the high black woods behind, were remembered now. Soon afterwards he had returned to the house, and again and again, avowedly to see Emily. In the late summer they used to walk out after the haymaking was all over, while the nightjar sang and the woods were dark and discreet and the sky above them as pale green as a new-mown field. They went in amongst the untrodden bracken together. He could recall the smell of the crushed fronds where they sat, the light of the near planet between the fox-gloves gushing from the violet sky, and the kisses that were as sweet as the honeysuckle overhanging them, and, unlike that, could be tasted again and again without cloying.

And now the cold whine of the wind in the roof and the drop of the rain, and Emily was lying at home, sick, with a dead new-born child in the next room, and a child that he was glad was dead, yes! that even she would not be crying after if she knew what a monstrous mistaken thing had come into the world with their help. Weekes looked at that old farmhouse and the rickyard, the crushed bracken bower, as if to search among these things engraved by joy upon his brain for the devilish magic that had brought about this wretchedness. He looked at her remembered face, scanning it for something to explain this thing, looked closely and fiercely at the face that was turned back towards him in her father's doorway so that he loved her from that day. What? Why? But neither in the young girl nor in the worn woman could he see what he sought. He thought of their labours, of the six children she had borne and reared, of her rough hands and wrenched voice, of the smearing out of all her prettiness except her hair. He turned it over and over, ruminating, undisturbed by the spurting of the milk into the pail, the trickle of the shower, or the sight of the hills and the clouds over the hills. Yet he did not take his eyes off these hills, nor change the look given to them by his pain and questioning – questioning he knew not what now – the whole order of things, perhaps, from which the terror had sprung unexpected. Having naught for his brain to grip and hold, but only the dead ghastly child lying still, and repeating the question, and round about it the moving world of men and Nature, enormous and endless and careless, each effort was weaker than the last and sorrow brought its narcotic stupidity. It was some time after he had drawn her last milk that the cow licked his face impatiently. He kicked away the stool and began singing a verse of a ribald song which he did not know he had remembered –

> Poor Sally's face is plain
> > But Sally's heart is kind –

And it was so singing that, without wishing it, he returned the question to the teeming womb and grave of the earth, to be swallowed up in the vast profusion of life and death, while the merry maid waved to and fro the coloured silks of the sunshine and of the rain, and the titmouse crept through the hedge, crying, waggishly, 'Fitchy! fitchy!'

*THE SHIP OF SWALLOWS: A SELECTION OF SHORT STORIES,*
*ed. Jeremy Hooker, 2005*

MICHAEL LONGLEY

from *A Jovial Hullabaloo**

Edward Thomas was killed by a shell-blast at the Battle of Arras in April 1917. Other geniuses died in the Great War: Wilfred Owen, Isaac Rosenberg, Charles Sorley. I revere these lost soldier-poets as well as those who survived the slaughter – Siegfried Sassoon, Robert Graves, Edmund Blunden, Ivor Gurney. It is wrong to confine such writers to the dubiously simplified category of war poet. When I read a poem like Owen's 'Insensibility' or Rosenberg's 'Dead Man's Dump' –

> None saw their spirits' shadow shake the grass,
> Or stood aside for the half used life to pass
> Out of those doomed nostrils and the doomed mouth –

when I read lines like these I picture the young Sophocles and the young Aeschylus trudging under the weight of their kitbags through the terrible mud.

In terms of scale there is no way we can compare the Troubles with the industrialised devastation of the Great War. But I am reminded of the War Poets when I consider my contemporaries and our apprenticeships in a damaged society. Owen's desperate desire to befriend and impress Sassoon feels familiar to me; as does the poetic transformation that Sassoon's (and Graves's) encouragement brought about in Owen's writing. After the war Graves and Sassoon befriended and helped Edmund Blunden; and then, in his turn, Blunden edited collections of Wilfred Owen's and Ivor Gurney's poems. As they tried to make sense of the nightmare of the trenches the War Poets were listening to each other.

In the early 1970s poets here were as dumbfounded as most people by the ferocity of the violence. Seamus Heaney has written of the 'search for images and symbols adequate to our predicament.' And in 1971, in a survey of the arts in Ulster called *Causeway*, I suggested that the poet 'would be inhuman if he did not respond to tragic events in his own community and a poor artist if he did not seek to endorse that response imaginatively . . .'

I added that the poet 'needs time in which to allow the raw material of experience to settle to an imaginative depth . . . He is not some sort of super-journalist commenting with unfaltering spontaneity on events immediately after they have happened. Rather, as Wilfred Owen stated, it is the poet's duty to warn . . .'

In such monumental poems as 'Easter 1916', 'Meditations in Time of Civil War', 'Nineteen Hundred and Nineteen', W. B. Yeats loomed large, an inescapable exemplar. More than any other poet he helped us to find our way through the minefield. Like Wilfred Owen in the trenches, Yeats demonstrated that the complex, intense lyric is capable of encompassing extreme experience:

> Now days are dragon-ridden, the nightmare
> Rides upon sleep: a drunken soldiery
> Can leave the mother, murdered at her door,
> To crawl in her own blood, and go scot-free . . .

We did not write in Yeats's shadow, as some would have it, but in the lighthouse beam of his huge accomplishment.

To be a poet is to be alive to both precursors and contemporaries. As regards my contemporaries from Northern Ireland, this may have been so in a further sense as poets here, with their different backgrounds and perspectives, reacted to the Troubles. Poems are aware of each other. No poem is a solo flight. In his wonderful lyric 'The Friendship of Young Poets', the Scottish poet Douglas Dunn conjures up an ideal scene:

> There is a boat on the river now, and
> Two young men, one rowing, one reading aloud.
> Their shirt sleeves fill with wind, and from the oars
> Drop scales of perfect river like melting glass.

The American poet and critic Randall Jarrell famously tells us: 'A good poet is someone who manages, in a lifetime of standing out in thunder-storms, to be struck by lightning five or six times; a dozen or two dozen times and he is great.' And Rilke says somewhere: 'You ought to wait and gather sense and sweetness for a whole lifetime . . . and then, at the very end, you might perhaps be able to write ten good lines.' The enterprise often feels like a long wait for something that does not necessarily happen. In 'How Poetry Comes to Me' the American Gary Snyder writes a poem about writing a poem:

It comes blundering over the
Boulders at night, it stays
Frightened outside the
Range of my campfire
I go to meet it at the
Edge of the light

It is mysterious why some people write good poems and then stop; and mysterious why others persist. I think being a poet is different from being a writer. Some poets are writers as well but they are usually protecting a core. Poetry can't be created to order. You can't write your way out of a poetic block. I have no idea where poetry comes from, or where it goes when it disappears. Silence is part of the enterprise.

*A JOVIAL HULLABALOO, 2008*

SEBASTIAN BARRY

# from *The Temporary Gentleman**

*Jack McNulty's Minute-Book*
 1957
 *A Prologue of Sorts*

'It's a beautiful night and no mistake. You would never think there was a war somewhere.'

These less than prophetic words were spoken by a young navy second-lieutenant, on the wide, night-bedarkened deck of our supply ship, bound for Accra. He was a tubby little man, whom the day's sun had scorched red. Happy to hear an Irish accent I asked him where he was from and he said, with that special enthusiasm Irish people reserve for each other when they accidentally meet abroad, Donegal. We talked then about Bundoran in the summer, where my father had often brought his band. It was a pleasure to shoot the breeze with him for a few moments as the engines growled on dimly, deep below, as if we were ferrying lions.

Oftentimes the greatest pleasure is to be had from nothing, or next to nothing. It is one of the delights of soldiering.

The cargo in fact was eight hundred men and officers, all headed for various parts of British Africa. There was the noise of the little parliaments of the card-players, and the impromptu music-halls of the whisky drinkers, and true enough a lovely mole-gray air moved across the ship in a beneficent wave. We could see the coast of Africa lying out along a minutely fidgeting shoreline. The only illuminations were the merry lights of the ship, and the sombre philosophical lights of God above. Otherwise the land ahead was favoured only by darkness, a confident brushstroke of rich, black ink.

I had been in an excellent mood for days, having picked the winner of the Middle Park Stakes at Nottingham. Every so often, I stuck a hand in my right pocket and jingled part of my winnings in the shape of a few half crowns. The rest of it was inserted into an inside pocket of my uniform – a fold of lovely crisp white banknotes. I'd got up to Nottingham on a brief furlough, having been given a length of time not quite long enough to justify the long trek across England and Ireland to Sligo. I know part of my happiness was in having escaped the storm and sickness of Mai – but I did not say that to myself at the time.

France had fallen to Hitler, and suddenly, bizarrely, colonies like the Gold Coast were surrounded by the new enemy, the forces of the Vichy French. No one knew what was going to happen, but we were being shunted down quickly to be in place to blow bridges, burst canals, and break up roads, if the need arose. We had heard the colonial regiments were being swelled by new recruits, thousands of Gold Coast men rushing to defend the Empire. I suppose this was when Tom Quaye, though of course I didn't know him then, joined up.

So I was standing there, flush with my winnings, not thinking of much, as always somewhat intoxicated by being at sea, somewhat in love with an unknown coast line, and the intriguing country lying in behind. I had also about a bottle of Scotch whisky in me, though I stood rooted as a tree for all that. It was a moment of simple exhilaration. My red hair, the selfsame red hair that had first brought me to the attention of Mai, for it was not I who said hello to her first, but she, with her sardonic question in the simple neat quadrangle of the university, 'I suppose you put a colour in that?' – my red hair was brushed flat back from my forehead, my second-lieutenant's cap holding it down like a pot lid, my cheeks had been shaved by my batman Percy Welsh, my underclothes were starched, my trousers were creased, my shoes were signalling back brightly to the moon – when suddenly the whole port side of the ship seemed to go up, right in front of my eyes, an enormous gush and geyser of water, a shuddering explosion, an ear-numbing rip of metallic noise, and a vast red cornet of flames the size of the torch on the Statue of Liberty. The young second-lieutenant from Donegal was suddenly as dead as one of those porpoises you will see washed up on the beach at Enniscrone after a storm, on the deck beside me, felled by a jagged missile of stray metal. Men came tearing up from below, the doorways oozing out men as if so much boiling molasses; there were cries and questions even as the gigantic fountain of displaced water collapsed and found the deck, and hammered us flat there as if we were blobs of dough. Two lads of my sappers were trying to peel me back up from the deck, itself splintered and cratered from the force, and now other stray bits of the ship rained down, clattering and banging and boasting and killing.

'That was a fucking torpedo,' said my sergeant, with perfect redundancy, a little man called Ned Johns from Cornwall, the most knowledgeable man for a fuse on an UXB I ever worked with. He probably knew the make and poundage of the torpedo, but if he did he didn't say. The next second the huge ship started to pitch to port, and before I could grab him, Ned Johns went off sliding down the new slope and smashing into the rail, gathered himself, stood up, looked back at me, and then was wrenched across the rail and out of view. I knew we were holed deep under the waterline, I could more or less feel it in my body, something vital torn out of the ship echoed in the pit of my stomach, some mischief done, deep, deep in some engine room or cargo-hold.

My other helper, Johnny 'Fats' Talbott, a man so lean you could have used him for spare wire, as poor Ned Johns once said, in truth was using me now as a kind of bollard, but that was no good, because the ship seemed to make a delayed reaction to its wound, and shuddered upward, the ship's-rail rearing up ten feet in a bizarre and impossible movement, catching poor John completely off guard, since he had been bracing himself against a force from the other direction, and off he went flying behind me, pulling the trouser leg off my uniform as he did so, sending my precious half-crowns firing in every direction.

So for a moment of odd calm I stood there, one leg bare to the world, my cap still in place inexplicably, myself drenched so thoroughly I felt myself to be one hundred per cent seawater. An iron ladder full of men, from God knows where, maybe even from inside the ship, or from the side of the command deck more likely, with about a dozen calling and screaming persons clinging to it like forest monkeys, moved past me as if it were a trolley being wheeled by the demon of this attack, and crossed the ravaged deck, and pitched down into the moiling, dark sea behind. Everything roared for that moment, the high night sky of blankening stars, the great and immaculate silver serving-dish of the sea itself, the rended ship, the offended and ruined men – and then, precipitatively, a silence reigned, the shortest reign of any silence in the empires of silence, the whole vista, the far-off coast, the deck, the sea, was as still for a moment as a painting, as if someone had just painted it all in his studio, and was gazing at it, contemplating it, reaching out to put a finishing touch on it, of smoke, of fire, of blood, of water, and then I felt the whole ship leave me, sink under my boots so suddenly that there was for that second a gap between me and it, so that wasn't I like an angel, a winged man suspended. Then gravity insisted I follow, gravity broke the spell, gravity ruined the bloody illusion, and I went miserably and roaringly downward with the ship, the deck broke into the waters, it smashed through the sacred waters like a child breaks an ice puddle in a Sligo winter, it made a noise like that, of something solid, something icy breaking, glass really, but not glass, infinitely soft and receiving water, the deeps, the dreaded deeps, the reason why fishermen never learn to swim, let the waters take us quickly, let there be no thrashing and hoping and swimming, no, let your limbs go, be calm, put your trust in God, pray quick to your Redeemer, and I did, just like an Aran fisherman, and gave up my soul to God, and sent my last signal of love flying back across Europe to Mai, Mai, and my children, up the night-filthied coast of Africa, across the Canaries, across the old boot of England and the ancient baby-shape of Ireland, I sent her my last word of love, I love thee, I love thee, Mai, I am sorry, I am sorry. Then the ocean closed over my head with its iron will, and the fantastical suck of the sinking ship drew me down as if a hundred demons were yanking on my legs, down down we went, our handsome troop-ship made in Belfast, the loose bodies of the already drowned, the myriad papers and plans for war, the tins of sardines we had taken in in Algiers, the fabulous matériel, the brand-new trucks, the stocks of tyres, the fifty-three horses, the wooden stakes, the planks, the boxes of carefully stored explosives, all down down to Neptune we went, extinguished in a moment without either glory or cowardice, an action of the Gods, of queer physics, that huge metal mass sucker-punched, beaten, ruined, wrecked, fucked to all hell as Ned Johns would say, and I felt the water all around as if I were in the body of a physical creature, as if this were its blood, and the scientifically-explainable forces at work were its sinews and muscles. And it stopped my mouth and found the secret worm-whorls of my ears, and it wanted entry into me, but I had grabbed, stolen, fetched out with an

347

instinctive exuberance, a last great gulp of breath, and I was bearing this down with me, in my chest, around my heart, as my singing response, my ears were now thundering with the thunders of the sea, I thought I could hear the ship itself cry out in a crazy vocabulary of pain, as if a man could learn this lingo somewhere, the tearing death-cries of a vessel. All the while as if still standing on the deck, but that was not possible, and then I thought the ship was turning sideways, like a giant in its bed, and I had no choice but to go with it, I was like a trout in its altered river after rain, or a salmon looking for the seam in a waterfall, where it could grip its way to the gravel-beds on grips of mere water, and now I thought I was rushing over the side, away from the deck, accelerated by some unknown force faster than the ship itself, and I was scraping along metal; I felt long sea-grass and barnacles, surely I could not have, but I thought I did, and just as the ship went right over, or so I imaged it, how could I know, in the deepest dark, the darkest deepest dark that ever was on the earth, an instance of utter blankness, violent movement, suddenly I felt the very keel of the troopship, something wide and round and good, the sacred keel, the foundation of the sailor's hope, the guarantor of his sleep between watches, but all up the wrong way, in the wrong place, violently torn from its proper place, and just in that moment, just in that moment, with a great groan, a weird and menacing sighing, a sort of silence as the worst noise in creation, the keel halted and went back the other way, like the spine of a whale, as if the ship was now fish, and because I was (without in any way intending to) holding on to the keel, riding it, like a fly on a saddle, it sort of threw me back the other way, catapulted me slowly, Mr Cannonball himself in the tuppenny circus of old at Enniscrone, my childhood flaring in my head, my whole life flaring, and then I seemed to be in the shrouds of the little forward mast, and I squeezed my body into a tight ball, again pure instinct, not a thought in my mind, and as the killed ship rolled slowly over, seeking its doom at least in a balletic and beautiful curve, the furled sails rolled me over and over, giving me strange speed, volition unknown, and I unfolded myself, like a lover rising victorious from the marriage bed, and I spread my arms, and I thrashed them into the ocean, and swam, and swam, looking for the surface, praying for it, gone a mile beyond mere breathlessness, ready to grow gills to survive this, and then it was there, the utterly simple sky, God's bare lights, in the serene harbours of the constellations, and I grabbed like a greedy child, like a maniac of greediness, onto a floating something, a shard of something, a ruined and precious fragment, and there I floated, gripping on, half-mad, for a minute without memory, oh Mai, Mai, for a minute all absence and presence, a creature blanked out and destroyed, a creature bizarrely renewed.

By the grace of God we were travelling in convoy that night. And by the grace of God, for some reason only known to its captain and its crouching sailors, the submarine melted off into the deeps, not that any of us saw it. A corvette bristling with machine-guns motored up near me, I heard the confident voices with wild gratitude, arms reached down into the darkness for me, pulled me from the chaos, and I slumped, suddenly lumpish and exhausted, at the boots of my rescuers, falling down to lie with other survivors, some with dark-blooded wounds, a few entirely naked, the clothes sucked off them.

I lay there, ticking with life, triumphant, terrified. I noticed myself checking my inside pocket for the roll of banknotes, as if watching someone else, as if I were two people, and I laughed at my other self for his foolishness.

And we steamed into Accra the following morning.


*THE TEMPORARY GENTLEMAN, 2013*

DENTON WELCH

# from *A Voice through a Cloud* *

I heard a voice through a great cloud of agony and sickness. The voice was asking questions. It seemed to be opening and closing like a concertina. The words were loud, as the swelling notes of an organ, then they melted to the tiniest wiry tinkle of water in a glass.

I knew that I was lying on my back on the grass; I could feel the shiny blades on my neck. I was staring at the sky and I could not move. Everything about me seemed to be reeling and breaking up. My whole body was screaming with pain, filling my head with its roaring, and my eyes were swimming in a sort of gum mucilage. Rich clouds of what seemed to be a combination of ink and velvet soot kept belching over me, soaking into me, then melting away. Bright little points glittered all down the front of the liquid man kneeling beside me. I knew at once that he was a policeman, and I thought that, in his official capacity, he was performing some ritual operation on me. There was a confusion in my mind between being brought to life – forceps, navel-cords, mid-wives – and being put to death – ropes, axes and black masks; but whatever it was that was happening, I felt that all men came to this at last. I was caught and could never escape the terrible natural law.

'What is your name? Where do you live? Where were you going?' the policeman kept asking. I could hear the fright in his voice. The fright made the voice more cruel and hard and impatient. I realized that he had been asking me these questions for a long time, and I told myself that I must give him the right answers at once, that I could think quite clear bloodless sentences, if I tried.

The words came out of my mouth. Some of them were slightly incorrect, others a little fantastic. I knew this, but felt that I had no real control over the words, and if I tried to repeat them again soberly they would arrange themselves in a still more grotesque pattern.

And as the shaken policeman bent over me, trying to take down my words, I felt the boiling and seething rise in me. It was drowning my brain, beating on it, plunging over it, shattering it. The earth swung, hovered, leaving my feet in the air and my head far below. I was overcome and drowned in waves of sickness and blackness . . .

*A VOICE THROUGH A CLOUD, 2004*

MICHAEL HAMBURGER

from *The Take-Over*\*

One morning, after breakfast, the telephone voice tells me that I'm to be taken to the Director. I have time to change, but refrain from putting on a suit. To appear casual is the least I can do. The Director, too, is casual, or appears so; rises not from a seat at a desk – I forget that writing has been abolished – but from an easy chair; shakes my hand, offers me another chair, but paces the room as he talks. I seem to recognize him, without being able to put a name to the face. Then the circumstances come back to me: a successful arms dealer, rarely mentioned in public, but briefly interviewed once for a documentary programme, and eloquent enough about his activities to have left an impression. The name is still a blur – no more than two vowel sounds, making a spondee. The twinkling eyes – less fanatical than those of other 'leaders' – ought to reassure me. They don't. Intelligence, in a man with his ambitions, is more formidable than fanaticism. 'So here we are,' he says unnecessarily. 'I'm sorry that I couldn't see you sooner. Perhaps I'd better begin by removing any possible misunderstanding. The words "court fool", I'm told, were used to prepare you for your employment. You'd better ignore the title – a mere *faute de mieux*, I assure you. No, your function is unprecedented and unique. It is to replace the written word, and all those liberal, humane and individualistic "values" once associated with it. As you know, I have had no choice but to ban it – and them – from the public sphere; but I am determined not to make the same mistakes as my historical predecessors. Which of them could afford the luxury of an opposition? You are to be my opposition – at complete liberty to say whatever is on your mind. And there's no need for you to clown, to be funny, when you're not in the mood. Amusement of so high an order is in the eye of the beholder, as it were. Your business is only to be truthful, by your lights. You can be Polonius rather than Feste, sententious rather than witty. Nothing is banned in our sessions, not even religion, though that, too, has had to be publicly proscribed, beyond those externals of observance which have been almost correctly described as "the opium of the people". "Bromide of the people", would be more accurate, since it doesn't hallucinate. Your special knowledge of literature is another qualification. You shall be my mobile museum, the live depository of dead cultures.' Silence. A long silence. He looks me in the eyes. 'Call me Jack, by the way. There is to be no formality between us.' That's the last straw. I am to be denied the distance of subordination, of deference. At last I blurt out: 'You're making a big mistake – Jack. You've got the wrong man. I've forgotten absolutely every-thing I ever read – except the things I learned by heart at school, Latin tags, some lines of verse, a date or two. And I'm completely tongue-tied in company, always have been. Couldn't bear to read out my stuff – let alone extemporize anything. If I was ever witty on paper, that was because the theme generated wit. And goodness knows where the themes come from. They were simply there, inside me. Not imposed on me from the outside, like the spontaneity you demand. Get rid of me now, or you'll regret it.' He laughed. 'Excellent, excellent. An excellent start. You've only to keep that up, and I shall be constantly entertained. Tongue-tied indeed! Forgotten everything! Just wait till you see what real illiteracy, real amnesia are like. We're experts in the art of inducing them.' 'Bless you, Jack,' I answer, inadvertently falling into my new rôle. 'All the kids will love you for that. You're the answer to every hippie's and pop fan's prayer.' He doesn't laugh at that. I can feel that I'm dismissed – for the day.

The routine takes over. Day after day I walk in the grounds, never to meet the King again. Most days a dumb official escorts me to the 'presence'. I've taken to solitary drinking, but the whisky could be lemon-ade, for all the effect it has on me. The more the Director tells me about his reconditioning programme, his agents in foreign countries busy creating power vacuums everywhere, his tightening stranglehold on the world commodity market, the re-employment, one by one, of the few people I used to respect, the less capable I become of serious comment. Tomfoolery is my only refuge. There were times when I responded to his boasting with harangues, protests, appeals. I recall those outbursts with shame. They served only to titillate his frivolity, which is limitless compared to mine, because his manipulations and machinations become other people's realities. 'I alone have succeeded in abolishing the past,' he brags. 'I shall leave no future that isn't a continuation of my presence; no going back, and no starting from scratch.' I salute him: 'Yes, indeed, your Nothingness, sir. Like the founder of the Millennial Reich that lasted a dozen years. He also tried to recreate the world in his image, which was nothingness, so as to usurp God's attributes, and nature's; until the people for whom he had "sacrificed" himself proved unworthy of him, because they couldn't see how endless subtraction could amount to anything but zero . . .' I goose-step round the room, then collapse on the floor. He chuckles. 'Kids' stuff, as well you know. More vulgarly monumental than Bismarck's Reich, and full of built-in atavisms. Killing off its own population, instead of putting it to good use. There hasn't been a single execution under my rule, not even of a so-called criminal. And I shall achieve my objective without a single military action.' I lower my head and charge. He tries to step aside, but has to use his hands to break the impact. It's my turn to laugh. 'Jack, Jack, the joker in the pack. Never dirties his hands, but mustn't turn his back.' He rings the bell. For the guards? No, for my dumb escort.


*THE TAKE-OVER, 2000*

SAMUEL BECKETT

# The North

Seen from below the wall presents an unbroken surface all the way round and up to the ceiling. And yet its upper half is riddled with niches. This paradox is explained by the levelling effect of the dim omnipresent light. None has ever been seen to seek out a niche from below. The eyes are seldom raised and when they are it is to the ceiling. Floor and ceiling bear no sign or mark apt to serve as a guide. The foot of the ladders pitched always at the same points leave no trace. The same may be said of the skulls and fists dashed against the wall. Even did such marks exist the light would prevent their being seen. The climber making off with his ladder to plant it elsewhere relies largely upon feel. He is seldom out by more than an inch or two and never by more than a few feet at the most because of the way the niches are disposed. On the spur of his passion his agility is such that even this deviation does not prevent him from gaining the nearest if not the desired niche and thence though with greater labour from regaining the ladder for the descent. There does none the less exist a north in the guise of one of the vanquished or better one of the women vanquished or better still the woman vanquished. She squats against the wall with her head between her knees and her legs in her arms. The left hand clasps the right shin-bone and the right the left forearm. The red hair tarnished by the light hangs to the ground. It hides the face and whole front of the body down to the crutch. The left foot is crossed on the right. She is the north. She rather than some other among the vanquished because of her greater fixity. To one bent for once on taking his bearings she may be of help. For the climber averse to avoidable acrobatics a given niche may lie so many paces or feet to east or west of the woman vanquished without of course his naming her thus or otherwise even in his thoughts. It goes without saying that only the vanquished hide their faces though not without exception. Standing or sitting with head erect some are content simply to open their eyes no more. It is of course forbidden to withhold the face or other part of the body from the searcher who demands it and who may without fear of resistance remove the hand from the flesh it hides or raise the lid to examine the eye. Among the searchers there are those who join the climbers with no thought of climbing and simply in order to inspect at close hand one or more among the vanquished or sedentary. The hair of the woman vanquished has thus many a time been gathered up and drawn back and the head raised and the face laid bare and all the front of the body down to the crutch. The inspection once completed it is usual to put everything carefully back in place as far as possible. It is enjoined by a certain ethics not to do unto others what coming from them might give offence. This precept is largely observed in the cylinder in so far as it does not jeopardize the search which would clearly be the merest mockery if in case of doubt it were not possible to check certain details. Direct action with a view to their elucidation is generally reserved for the persons of the sedentary and vanquished. Face or back to the wall these normally offer but a single aspect and so may have to be turned the other way. But wherever there is motion as in the arena or among the watchers and the possibility of encompassing the object there is no call for such manipulations. There are times of course when a body has to be brought to a stand and disposed in a certain position to permit the inspection at close hand of a particular part or the search for a scar for example or a birthmark. To be noted finally the immunity in this respect of those queuing for a ladder. Obliged for want of space to huddle together over long periods they appear to the beholder a mere jumble of mingled flesh. Woe betide the rash searcher who carried away by his passion dare lay a finger on the least among them. Like a single body the whole queue falls on the offender. Of all the scenes of violence the cylinder has to offer none approaches this.

*THE NORTH, 1972*

356

EDWARD UPWARD

## Sunday

I am going back to lunch. There is no ambush, no one will ask me to show an entrance ticket, I have not tampered with the motor-mower, no butcher-boy has chalked my name on the basin of the fountain. This is a public path, no discrimination is made against persons not moving on a definite errand, against women without tennis shoes, men who aren't easily called Freddy by their colleagues. I have as much right to walk here as anyone. I am invited, everyone is invited, we are expected to stop and look at the mandarin ducks, to use the less direct path up the side of the valley, smell the lupins, poke groundsel through the wire meshes of the aviary. Why did the council put flood-lights in the trees round the fountain and build a thatched hut for the ducks on an island? Not merely in order to give the contract to their friends or because it's the fashion, but also because they want the town to have a good name with visitors. That's what civic consciousness really means, and it's a perfectly sound business proposition I suppose. They are really gratified that people come here, we are doing them a service, all kinds of people, dwarfs with diseases, young men with temporary jobs in the town, airmen and sailors, old women and public schoolboys returning from church, girls. There will be no inquisition at the park gates, no one is curious about your face, it is quite unnecessary to cross the grass in order to avoid seeming to follow the women who happen to be walking in front of you. Probably no one here knows anyone else. And suppose someone who did know you came up to you and suddenly asked what you were doing, you could say quite naturally 'I am going for a walk' or 'I am looking at the ducks'. You wouldn't have to pretend that you were exercising a terrier or going to buy a Sunday newspaper. That's the advantage of a place like this in a large town. There's no need to suspect that people are watching you from behind window curtains and wondering what you are doing. If anyone looks at you, you can see that he is looking at you, and you know he thinks you are merely walking through the park. And suppose everyone here were actually staring at me, suppose I were dancing or wearing sensible clothes, I should probably feel rather exhilarated. But as it happens I shall not be accused of anything, there is no kind of danger, not the least need to want to escape like a cat under the laurel bushes. I can't even flatter myself that I'm ill.

I am going back to my lodgings for lunch. Who will be there? Only the table, the flower with protruding stamens arching from its jug like a sabre-toothed tiger, the glass of custard, pleated apple-green satin behind the fretwork fleur-de-lis panel of the piano. The whole afternoon and evening will be free. Realize that, realize what I could do. All the possibilities of thinking and feeling, exploration and explanation and vision, walking in history as among iron and alabaster and domes, focusing the unity of the superseded with the superseding, recognizing the future, vindicating the poets, retiring between pillars as Socrates, desperate as Spartacus, emerging with Lenin, foreseeing the greatest of all eras. But unless I am very careful I shall sit on the sofa trying to decide not to go on reading the paper. I shall look out of the window. People will pass carrying neatly rolled umbrellas and after tea bells will toll. Everyone will appear quite at ease, fairly well-dressed, comfortably married, not at all furtive or sinister. Nothing will visibly suggest that they are all condemned, that what they stand for is already dead, putrescent, stinking, animated only by preying corpse-worms. I shall begin to doubt whether they are dead, whether it's not merely my own inefficiency which vomits when I hear them hint: 'In this funny old world of ours one must be a realist.' Hypocrisies which during the week seemed irrelevant abstractions will palpably promenade, bow, exchange smiles. I shall suspect that my work has been a drug, that all the week I have evaded this reality, that in future my leisure – the gaps between drug-takings – will become more and more impossible to bear. And the drug itself will never be anticipated with pleasure, it will always be feared. Perhaps that's why I've got nervous diarrhoea now. I feel as though I were in a waiting-room. Tomorrow I have to use a rotary duplicator for the first time.

Ah-ha, we are getting nearer to it now, we are becoming quite daring. The modest little secret has popped out at last. Now we are in our birthday suit. Oh, look, mother, there are spots all over his back. So that's why he was explaining that sunbathing permanently injures the brain cells. Is it credible? Yes, I am vulgarly anxious about my work. All other explanations are mainly decorative, shamming a greater horror, demon masks to divert attention. I am afraid that I shall not be able to understand the mechanism of the duplicator, that I shall not know how to fit the stencil on to the roller, I shall not get through what I have to do in time, shall perhaps damage the machine, be warned that my work must improve. Unless I am very careful I shall spend the whole of this afternoon uselessly trying to elaborate my fear into something monumental and flattering, and in the end quite frankly thinking of tomorrow.

Epictetus advised contempt for all things not dependent on choice. What's the worst thing, excluding murder and arson, in which I might be implicated tomorrow? I might be sacked without a testimonial. Epictetus would tell me that this is something outside my control, that I ought to be ready to accept it without complaint if it comes, that I should set my heart only on things which no external accident can endanger. He forestalled the 'His will is our peace' idea in less mystical language. Of course the idea is useless now, worse than useless, dangerous, sinister. Whether I am sacked or not depends at least partly on whether I make up my mind to understand the mechanism of the duplicator. I can't just forbid myself to be seriously interested in the success or failure of the copies, and then, if they fail, highmindedly submit to a thrashing from a slave-owner. No one would attempt to thrash or torture me, I should simply be asked to find another job. And if I found one the same process would begin over again, till in the end I should have no job at all. Things may have been different under the feudal barons. Then you were someone's property and you might be thrashed but you wouldn't be abandoned. That's what gave colour to the God the Father theory. But today real passivity is only possible to the leisured. Nevertheless there are thousands of people even now with jobs in this town who are made miserable by the idea that they ought to be at peace with their own souls. Though it's true they may not formulate it to themselves quite in that way – they may feel remorse for hating their wives, or they may wear an enamelled badge with the inscription 'Prepare to meet thy God', or they may make useless resolves to do their work at the office cheerfully. And what happens if they succeed in doing their work cheerfully? Suppose I became cheerful, suppose I refused to be alarmed by the duplicator. Then very soon I should be put on to something more difficult. And suppose even then I didn't revolt – I should soon be put on to something more difficult still. And in the end I shouldn't be a subordinate at all. I should have become one of those responsible liars and twisters who make a profit out of believing that drudgery and servility ought to be accepted cheerfully. But I am not likely to reach that position. I am much nearer to those other blunderers who, cynically regarding as a dishonour and a horror the work they have to do every day, try to preserve the old integrity intact within the blind enclosure of their minds. That is the maddest mistake of all.

It is mad to be content to hate every external danger, to be an ostrich, to accept any explanation which minimizes the importance of material gains or losses, to fail to try to find a real solution. It's no use pretending you are splendidly or redeemingly or even interestingly doomed. If you are doomed at all, and it is still possible for you not to be one of those who are doomed, you are doomed like a factory which excludes the latest machinery or like a migratory bird which fails to migrate. Don't flatter yourself that history will die or hibernate with you; history will be as vigorous as ever but it will have gone to live elsewhere. No, you are not a martyr, you are not a conqueror, you recognize that, you are aware that only history which is already living elsewhere can make martyrs and afterwards conquerors. Then where is it living, how can you get to it? Can it have disguised itself as a rotary duplicator, as traffic fussing in a smelly street, as electricity, as lying advertisements, as dingy and crowded tenements, as factory hooters, as any or all of those things which are so uneasily reflected on the surface of the old passivity? Stop just a moment. Aren't we becoming a little extravagant, almost metaphysical? Don't you think so? Because it's well-known that comfortably-paid university experts have warned us again and again against mistaking abstract generalizations for concrete things. Don't you suspect that after all they may have been right, that history is nothing more than a convenient figment, an abstraction, and that only concrete things like motor coaches and duplicators and ultimately electrons – which though not perceptible to the senses would be if they could – are real? And why not go one step farther, why not say that electrons and duplicators and motor coaches are nothing more than abstractions? Isn't that what you have been trying to convince yourself of all along? Day after day you have walked to work in the morning, trying not to feel sick, trying not to be degraded by petty fears, despising the genuine Jesus-gang who at least believed that evil was real, trying to dismiss the office buildings as an inconvenient dream, as a boring abstraction, as something neither pleasant nor unpleasant, without colour or shape or substance, finally as nothing at all – and every day you have failed completely. You have been jarred and stung beneath your pretences by the very reality which your pretences were designed to disguise. You have failed to deny history, as you always must fail until you are mad or dead.

History is here in the park, in the town. It is in the offices, the duplicators, the traffic, the nursemaids wheeling prams, the airmen, the aviary, the new viaduct over the valley. It was once in the castle on the cliff, in the sooty churches, in your mind; but it is abandoning them, leaving with them only the failing energy of desperation, going to live elsewhere. It is already living elsewhere. It is living in the oppression and hustle of your work, in the sordid isolation of your lodgings, in the vulgarity and shallowness of the town's attempts at art and entertainment, in the apprehensive dreariness of your Sunday leisure. History is living here, and you aren't able to die yet and you can't go mad.

But history will not always be living here. It will not always wear these sordid and trashy clothes. History abandoned the brutal fatherliness of the castle and it will abandon Sunday and the oppression of the office too. It will go to live elsewhere. It is going already to live with the enemies of suffering, of suffering beside which yours shows like silly hysteria, with people who are not content to suppress misery in their minds but are going to destroy the more obvious material causes of misery in the world. And the man who doesn't prefer suicide or madness to fighting – and how could anyone who has been at all near to suicide or madness prefer them? – will join with those people. He will look for history not in a Sunday afternoon's reading at his lodgings, not even in reading Lenin, nor in any of the excitements of thinking and feeling, but in the places where those people are. He will go back to his lodgings for lunch. He will read the newspaper, but not for more than a quarter of an hour. He will look out of the window and see the black hats and rolled umbrellas, but he will no longer be paralysed by disgust or apprehension. He will go out into the street and walk down to the harbour. He will go to the small club behind the Geisha Café. He will ask whether there is a meeting tonight. At first he may be regarded with suspicion, even taken for a police spy. And quite naturally. He will have to prove himself, to prove that he isn't a mere neurotic, an untrustworthy freak. It will take time. But it is the only hope. He will at least have made a start.

*A RENEGADE IN SPRINGTIME: SELECTED SHORT STORIES,*
*ed. Alan Walker, 2003*

CHRISTOPHER MIDDLETON

## Epilogue: The Gaze of the Turkish Mona Lisa

I could feel her gaze resting on me, so strangely, lightly, that it would have been inept to return it. She sat diagonally opposite, at a small square table, in this 'Iskender Kebap', or Alexander Grill. There she had settled with her sturdy husband and fat (anon hiccupping) son. Close as this family was to me at my identical table, their conversation, scant in any case, was almost inaudible. Me in my buff travelling shirt and white trousers, with my white beard, rather ragged, thinning brown hair, she was taking me in. While she'd been sitting down I had looked at her: a fleshy woman wearing a headscarf that spread across broad shoulders, a nondescript headscarf. Then, in an instant, I had noticed something about her lower lip. As she almost smiled, or pouted, a tiny crease appeared in it, a seamark on a horizon. I remembered the same crease which appeared now and then in Tana Cochran's lower lip, also halfway along the left half of it, whenever she looked rueful but was also taking me in. What sort of conspiracy might this be?

This Turkish woman's moon face would have looked heavy, too much flesh, if it had not been for her delicate features, the tilted planes of skin which pronounced those features, catching the light as she turned her head. Her eyes were not large, but lazy, inviting intimacy, the skin a rosy brown with a velvet texture, and now a gentle disdain, untainted by any bitterness, haunted her expression.

So she was not altogether submissive, and her face, her barn of a body (on this hot summer evening in an upstairs downscale Iskender Kebap), her body beneath all those swathes of light clothing, stored the woes and waves of a resistance that have for centuries shaped her function in the family – to oblige, but in the worst of times to bite every bullet, to provide at all times from the least resources. I did want to look into her face, wanted to show that I was not indifferent, not an object; but feeling her gaze on me, the stranger – perhaps she had never been so close to one of *them*, and an old one too – I chose not to do so. I actually resolved to let her look her fill, to make no move that might interrupt or deflect her gaze. I pretended to be entirely absorbed by my morsels of grilled chicken. Might she not be gazing at me as Louise Moillon gazed at her apricots, Cézanne at his cardplayers, Van Gogh at his boots, and Rilke at his fountain in Rome?

The grill, opposite the now twilit mosque, was apparently a focus for social events. Two young waiters were polishing glasses, rattling knives and forks, setting a long table for a feast. Sounds from the street: traffic, donkey carts, footsteps; for once, except for a faint throb of electronic drums, a pause in the usual assorted musics. And then, as if from the other end of the world, a derisory cackle, with a hoot for crescendo, broke through these habitual sounds, over and over, while a low voice, provoking it, warbled on and on. The Mona Lisa occupied the one segment of my auditory circle from which no sound was coming; this was also the one and only segment of my visual semicircle into which I forbade myself to look.

There was a good smell coming up from the embers of the fire in the downstairs window frame, where little folded knobs of chicken and lamb chops were being grilled, each run through with a wooden skewer: the stylus, I thought, which for aeons has inscribed into the subtext of Anatolian history the taste of meat. And still I sensed her eyes on me, so I wondered what she was making of him: 'Why alone? Where from? Can he speak? What is he looking for here in our town?' I was thinking, too, that downstairs sat another presence. It had loomed up out of a twilight as I had walked in: the silent wrinkled crone who reached out her hand to take your money. For how many years had she sat at her desk in that nook, blinking at numerals? But dovetailed into the deflection of my concern was 'his' thought: Who is this being? Does she suffer, that such sidereal spaciousness should contract itself into the gaze she is levelling at me? Does the little boy know what a radiance can break out of the meat of his mother?

Eventually, the Mona Lisa stood up to leave. She walked with a lazy shuffle, haunches swaying, not because she was heavy, but because that was the right way to walk, as if afloat, yet hardly lifting the feet, like a Navajo canyon woman (again, from below, the cackle and the hoot).

As she floated down the narrow staircase, following the boy and the husband, I saw her headscarf flutter a little and wanted more than ever to see her hidden face. She kept on walking, shuffle shuffle. I did not suppose that she felt my gaze on the back of her head, as I had for forty minutes felt hers on one side of mine.

That afternoon, at Pisidian Antioch, an hour's bus-ride to the south, I had walked over the outcrop of granite on which masons once constructed a temple of Augustus, to supersede a more ancient shrine, that of Kybele. Now the round Anatolian head of Kybele, enshrined in a nondescript headscarf, had disappeared, surely passing through a puff of wood-scented smoke at the foot of the stairs.

Yet of course we eluded each other, excluded each other. Her gaze, whether aesthetic or sexual, or both, as it were astride those two rungs in the ladder of her curiosity, had been scanning chiefly the right side of my head, and I'd had only a glimpse of her. And though I'd sensed her gaze, its aura, moving around me, I cannot guess to what extent she really fathomed me: besides, my interpretation of her had gone off along a mythical tangent.

Was I, to a woman most likely ignorant of 'art' as Westerners mean it, standing in for an art object? Not exactly. Stretch the analogy, even then, and here was a man being studied as if he were some sort of art object, by a person in whom that same man detected a resemblance to a woman immortalized five centuries before by Leonardo's painting. Yes, I had come to know, almost, how it felt to be held under the gaze of the Mona Lisa. Cackle and hoot forsooth! And the circles of analogy had multiplied: in the moment of such an 'aesthetic experience' your body has become an antenna for your dead, if you remember them. You have the experience for them, not only for yourself. You have become a feeler extended by those who can feel no more. Through images, with a whole heart, now, if you can, you do invoke them. For the record: as I sat there alone, I recalled a Madonna of the Rocks that presided over the Broadwood in my father's music room, and a Venus Anadyomene – her gaze, not quite focussed yet, would rest on the students who came for tea on Sundays. Her reflection appeared on the silverplate teapot when my mother tilted it.

That steady gaze of the Turkish Mona Lisa – no, I am supplying it, unless, steady as it seemed, I not only imagined but also sensed it – I did sense it by some means supplied by ancient powers she possessed, no marvel to her, powers of sensitive participation. So, even if I supply or not only imagine the gaze, she was unknowingly conjuring out of me a power to match her own. At least, she was animating me to participate in her gaze by interiorizing it.

This was hardly communication; or else it was – subdued and lopsided, but a communication of the isolated, as Montale has described it. If so, had I not got the richer share of it, a hint of 'the fatal isolation of each one of us'? Yet what a tenuous space for two beings to hoard their strangeness in – the diagonal across two small tables upstairs in a small grill in a small tattered town, with the enormous material spread of Anatolia on every side; a crushing weight of time, hot lake, freezing mountain, zoomed over, beneath, and around them, while they were secretly moving, moment by moment, across each other's independent lines of perception.

It is no wonder that principally women have challenged any aesthetic grounded in the attentive masculine gaze, wherever it might be directed. Men told themselves that the pictures they studied, poems they recited, spoke back to them in their chilled language, men's, and that a circuit could be completed by such intellectual participation, a judgment of value recorded. The gaze I had felt was liquid, light, calm, circumambient; touching, rather than probing, it reminded me that I had a heart with secret deeps of its own, a heart *in the clear*.

The gaze of the Turkish Mona Lisa, directed at me, her stranger-creature, all unknowingly, and my not shaking it off, but gladly receiving it, not yet recognizing it as a gaze aforetimes feared – called *fascinatio* – combined then to alleviate my doubt as to the resonance of the singular. Yet how mute the singular was, silenced by the cocksure chorus of generalizations. Speak out you must, if only to test the air, to define your opalescence, but who would appoint a paradise under a dunghill? If the use of knowledge was to straighten understanding, wasn't it also to animate it, to lift understanding up, straight off the ground?

Yes and no. Poetic understandings are, leastways, narrow unless grounded: earth means to have her say. They are grounded even in dry areas of knowledge, where only doggèd scavenging may release a trickle of poetry; grounded also – 'orphically' – in subterraneous torment. Corkscrew tracks, not straight ones, spell themselves out between you and the mountaintop. But the new Moloch, instantaneous information supplied readymade, cannot accommodate this Turkish Mona Lisa gaze, for the gaze dwells in a mobility that sustains the interval between knowledge dispersed all over the nervous system and the jet of a poetic word. Such a word originates in the *storage*, but its trajectory outside, its own velocity in time, depends on the nuances of its tone and the values that mobilize its freight. Significance, being subject to change, is some-thing emergent, minutely so, something also that disappears as if it were too volatile to be coerced by conscious powers of attention.

When art comes into this puzzle, it could be to show what mortality is not, to explore shimmering borderlands. On the vexed way to what eludes the gaze, it lives untroubled, made strangely of ourselves, across uttermost limits of recital.

Sometimes vaporizing those limits, so that dried-up things can be perceived afresh, pristine, in the condition of their emergence, it is Apollo when art, discharging frenzy, achieves balance. Economics and politics, from that distance, will have shrunk to pinpricks. A simultaneous concentration and diversification of language particles transforms all slack into energy; and the energy is all gaze, all myth, atmospheric, the imaginary, a radiance of the remotest chance to be glad for what you cannot possess, cannot territorialize. Old misery festers, old fear persists, and difference animates an increasingly nervous few. Yet from the gladness we learn not to mistake myth for contingency, and not to mark out, as Adversary or Angel, any other kind of unquelled ego who happens also to be passing by.

These, at least, were my afterthoughts in the night bus travelling south to the sea.


*CRYPTO-TOPOGRAPHIA: STORIES OF SECRET PLACES, 2002*

Julian Bell, *This Island, Now*, ink drawing from Brian Hinton's
*The Heart's Clockwork* (1990)

# Notes

Page 50, PROTHALAMION, David Jones. An author's note following the poem records that it was written 'between 10.30 pm and midnight on Thursday, September 12th, 1940, at 61 King's Road, Chelsea, London SW3'.

Page 52, *from* THE TESTAMENT OF CRESSEID, Seamus Heaney. These are the opening verses of Heaney's re-telling (with images by Hughie O'Donoghue) of the narrative poem written by the fifteenth-century Scottish makar Robert Henryson.

Page 54, *from* VENUS AND ADONIS, Ted Hughes. These are the closing verses of Hughes's translation of Ovid's *Venus and Adonis*. Published alongside that of *Salmacis and Hermaphroditus*, it was paired with drawings and an original etching by Christopher Le Brun, in *Shakespeare's Ovid*, published in aid of the Shakespeare Globe Trust and its appeal to rebuild the Globe Theatre.

Page 56, *from* THE BENDING OF THE BOW, Neil Curry. This is the ending of Curry's version of the closing books of Homer's *Odyssey*, published with images by Jim Dine.

Page 66, NOON, Michael Field. 'Michael Field' was the joint *nom de plume* of Katherine Bradley (1846–1914) and her niece Edith Cooper (1862–1913). When Edith's mother became a permanent invalid Katherine joined the Cooper household to help look after the children. Aunt and niece lived together as devoted companions: in collaboration they wrote twenty-seven tragedies and eight volumes of verse. They became Roman Catholics in 1907, and died of cancer within a year of each other.

Page 68, DEW, Simon Armitage. In 2012 Armitage was commissioned by the Ilkley Literature Festival to write site-specific poetry. 'Dew' is one of six poems composed on the poet's Pennine walks. *Stanza Stones* is a record of that journey: it includes contributions from Tom Lonsdale, a former Chief Landscape Architect for the City of Manchester, and the work of the letter-carver Pip Hall.

Page 74, LEGAL TENDER, Fred D'Aguiar. The poem comes from *I Have Found a Song*, a collection of poems and images published in 2010 to mark the bicentenary of the Abolition of the Slave Trade Act. Arts Council England commissioned twelve poets to write on the theme of enslavement. Interspersed with these are contributions by five artists invited by Enitharmon Editions to produce work on the same theme. The poem's title is also that of an earlier Enitharmon book, Deirdre Shanahan's first collection of poems (1988).

Page 81, RIDDLE, Stuart Henson. The answer is – a supermarket trolley.

Page 100, BREAK OF DAY IN THE TRENCHES, Isaac Rosenberg. This familiar version of the poem was subsequently amended by Jean Liddiard in her volume of Rosenberg's unpublished letters and poem versions, *Poetry Out of My Head and Heart* (Enitharmon Press, 2007), in the light of detailed textual research by Dr Vivien Noakes while preparing her definitive edition of *Isaac Rosenberg*, published by Oxford University Press in 2008.

Page 197, *from* OUT OF THE BLUE, Simon Armitage. Told from the point of view of an English trader working in the North Tower of the World Trade Centre, the poem-film *Out of the Blue* was commissioned by Channel 5 and broadcast five years after the 9/11 attacks on America. It won the 2006 Royal Television Society Documentary Award.

Page 210, BLUE SONG, Dannie Abse. Soon after the poem was published in his chapbook *In Extra Time*, Dannie Abse – inspired by David Hockney's exhibition of Yorkshire landscapes at the Royal Academy – wrote out a new stanza in Stephen Stuart-Smith's own copy of the book. It appears here for the first time.

Page 232, MALE FIGURE PLAYING A DOUBLE FLUTE, Richard Berengarten. The writer has changed his name: at the time of publication it was Richard Burns.

Page 238, RIDDLE, Kit Wright. The answer is – a pencil lead.

Page 239, *from* THIRTEEN WAYS OF LOOKING AT RILLIE, Edwin Morgan. This poem celebrates Jack Rillie, of whom Morgan wrote: 'Jack Rillie, now retired, was a very distinguished member of the English Department at Glasgow University, and divulged a broad humanism which would make it possible for us to enumerate more than thirteen ways of looking at such a finely exploratory mind. Several generations of students will testify to his brilliant but never pedantic qualities'.

Page 240, A DENT, Paul Muldoon. Dr Michael Allen (1936–2011), to whom the poem is dedicated, was a founding member of the Belfast Group of writers, which included Seamus Heaney, Bernard MacLaverty and Stewart Parker. As a senior lecturer in American and Irish literature at Queen's University, Belfast, he also numbered among his students the poets Paul Muldoon, Ciaran Carson and Medbh McGuckian.

Page 252, LEGEND HAS IT, Jane Griffiths. In an introduction, Jane Griffiths wrote: 'A number of things came together in writing this poem. I went back to my first responses to Edward Thomas, more than fifteen years ago. What struck me most then was – perhaps predictably – the story about his sudden transition from prose to poetry after a conversation with Robert Frost. I was delighted by it, but at the same time rather sceptical about the way the story had become almost better known than the writing. The other thing that greatly attracted me was Thomas's habit of looking at a house or a place as if it were the image of the perfect life – and his own questioning of that response.'

Page 305, THE DOOR THAT OPENS ON TWO SIDES, Kathleen Raine. Taken from *Faces of Day and Night*, a volume of memoirs and essays written in the early 1940s: apart from a few chapters published in periodicals, this Enitharmon 1972 publication was its first appearance in print.

Page 311, *from* MY YORKSHIRE, David Hockney. Maurice Payne, mentioned in the final paragraph, was born in 1937. A printer, he worked with Hockney on his etchings in the late 1960s and 1970s, as well as with many other artists including Jim Dine. Hockney made a number of portraits of him.

Page 324, *from* A KIND OF DECLARATION, David Gascoyne. This mock interview was written by Gascoyne for *Temenos 1* (1980).

Page 341, *from* A JOVIAL HULLABALOO, Michael Longley. This was Longley's inaugural lecture as Ireland Professor of Poetry, a position he held from 2007 to 2010.

Page 344, *from* THE TEMPORARY GENTLEMAN, Sebastian Barry. *The Temporary Gentleman* (Faber, 2013) is the third of Barry's novels to explore the history of the McNulty family. Enitharmon produced a signed limited edition of the book's first chapter, together with an introduction by the author.

Page 350, *from* A VOICE THROUGH A CLOUD, Denton Welch. Welch showed great promise as an artist, but in June 1935 he was knocked off his bicycle by a motorist, severely damaging his spine and kidneys: for the rest of his life he was a semi-invalid. This extract from his closely autobiographical novel records the fateful accident. *A Voice Through a Cloud*, not quite completed on his death in 1948 at the age of thirty-three, was first published in 1950 by John Lehmann.

Page 352, *from* THE TAKE-OVER, Michael Hamburger. At the start of the second paragraph, the king ('Day after day I walk in the grounds, never to meet the king again') refers to a brief encounter earlier in the story.

# ALAN CLODD
*Director 1967 to 1987*

Alan Clodd (1918–2002) was born in Dublin and educated in England. His grandfather, the Victorian rationalist, banker and writer Edward Clodd, was a close friend of Thomas Hardy, George Gissing and George Meredith, so literature was in the blood. After war service in the Second World War with the Friends' Ambulance Unit in Egypt and UNRAA in Italy, he worked for a bookseller and for five years at the London Library, before taking a succession of unsuitable clerical jobs with firms exporting luxury cars. In the 1960s he decided to turn his book-collecting hobby into a full-time career as both a publisher and book-dealer, testing the water by issuing poem pamphlets by Christopher Logue, Ronald Firbank and Kathleen Raine. In 1967, with Raine's encouragement, he established Enitharmon Press. It was significant that he should take its name from William Blake's prophetic works, for he regarded the truest poetry as romantic and visionary. Enitharmon swiftly became known for its fine-quality editions, many designed and printed by Eric Gill's nephew Christopher Skelton, and for the adventurousness of the list. In the early 1980s, looking for a younger successor, Clodd invited Stephen Stuart-Smith to take on the imprint from him, and this transition took place in 1986–87.

# STEPHEN STUART-SMITH
*Director 1987 to the present*

Stephen Stuart-Smith (b. 1954) began his career as a teacher, working from 1978 until 1989 in secondary schools in London and Hampshire, and for ten years directing a schools' poetry festival in the southern counties. At the invitation of Alan Clodd he began publishing under the Enitharmon Press imprint in 1987, his first book being Jeremy Hooker's *Master of the Leaping Figures*. In 2001 he founded Enitharmon Editions as a specialist publisher of *de luxe* artists' books. He was the first Chair of the Poetry School (1997–2003) and since 2016 has chaired the trustees of the Robert Anderson Research Charitable Trust. He is a Fellow of the Royal Society of Arts, a Fellow of the English Association, a member of AICA (Association Internationale des Critiques d'Art) and for a decade sang with the London Philharmonic Choir.

David Hockney, *Stephen Stuart-Smith*, camera lucida
drawing 1999 © David Hockney

# LAWRENCE SAIL

Lawrence Sail's *Waking Dreams: New & Selected Poems* (Bloodaxe Books, 2010) was a Poetry Book Society Special Commendation; his most recent collection is *The Quick* (Bloodaxe Books, 2015). Enitharmon has brought out a selection of his Christmas poems, *Songs of the Darkness* (2010), and *Cross-currents* (2005), a book of essays. He is a Fellow of the Royal Society of Literature.

Jeffrey Morgan, *Grasshopper*, wood engraving from
Michael Longley's *Wavelengths* (2009)

# Index of Writers, Translators and Artists

# Acknowledgements

Lawrence Sail, Enitharmon Press and Enitharmon Editions are most grateful to the following artists for permission to reproduce their work: Norman Ackroyd, Julian Bell, Tony Bevan, Sir Peter Blake, Glenn Brown, Sir Michael Craig-Martin, Jim Dine, Gilbert and George, Pip Hall, David Hockney, John Lawrence, Christopher Le Brun PRA, Duane Michals, Jeffrey Morgan, Hughie O'Donoghue, Dame Paula Rego, Erica Sail. Thanks are also due to Laura Staab of DACS, representing Tony Bevan; Estate of Cecil Collins; Sarah Williams, Estate of David Jones; Tracy Bartley, Estate of R. B. Kitaj; Estate of Victor Pasmore, Marlborough Fine Art; William Pryor and Charlotte Parsons, Raverat Ltd, Estate of Gwen Raverat (1885–1957), for permission to reproduce block cuts originally made for *Mountains and Molehills*.

We would also like to acknowledge the help given by: Chrissy Blake, Sebastian Carter, Thomas Dilworth, Glenys Johnson and Glenbevan Ltd, Martin Koffer (Gomer Press), Edgar Laguinia, Stan Lane (Gloucester Typesetting Services and Stonehouse Fine Press), Tom Lonsdale, Clare O'Donoghue, Sutchinda Rangsi Thompson, Frankie Rossi (Marlborough Fine Art), Roger Thorp and Amber Husain (Thames & Hudson), Dame Marina Warner, Peter Willberg.

We would also like to thank Julie Green (Head of Reproductions, David Hockney Inc.) and her colleague Robert Berg for generously providing the files reproduced on pages 207, 313 and 373:

David Hockney, *Rain on the Studio Window* (2009) from *My Yorkshire*, de luxe edition, 2011. Inkjet printed computer drawing on paper. Edition of 75, 22 × 17" © David Hockney. Photo credit: Richard Schmidt

David Hockney, *Summer Road Near Kilham* (2008). Inkjet printed computer drawing on paper. Edition of 25, 48 ¼ × 37" © David Hockney

David Hockney, *Stephen Stuart-Smith. London. 30th May 1999*. Pencil and coloured pencil on paper using a camera lucida, 15 × 14" © David Hockney. Photo credit: Richard Schmidt. Collection The David Hockney Foundation.

We owe a great debt to Susan Wightman and Michael Mitchell of Libanus Press, who have realised the overall concept of the cover and the design of the text and colour-plate sections, as well as acting as our main typographic designers since 2006.

Warm thanks are due to all the writers and translators whose work is reproduced in this anthology, and to the following: Estate of Dannie Abse; Benjamin Adams, Estate of Anna Adams; Dr R. V. Bailey, literary executor of U. A. Fanthorpe; Edward Beckett, Estate of Samuel Beckett; Estate of Frances Bellerby; Tom Cornford, Estate of Frances Cornford; Hilary Davies, literary executor of Sebastian Barker; Jennifer Dunbar Dorn, Estate of Ed Dorn; Faber & Faber Ltd; Raymond Foye, literary executor of John Wieners, and Robert Dewhurst; Lady Antonia Fraser; August Kleinzahler and Clive Wilmer, literary executors of Thom Gunn; Roger Garfitt, Estate of Frances Horovitz; Marie Heaney; Martin Hesketh and Catherine Robinson, Estate of Phoebe Hesketh; David Higham Ltd, representing the Estate of Edwin Brock; Jeremy Hill, Kenneth Haynes, Alice Goodman, Estate of Sir Geoffrey Hill; Carol Hughes; David Higham Ltd and the University of Texas, Estate of Denton Welch; David Higham Ltd and Luke Ingram, The Wylie Agency, for permission to reproduce the work of Jack Kerouac; Estate of Elizabeth Jennings; Brian Keeble, literary executor of Kathleen Raine; Estate of George MacBeth; Guthrie McKie, literary executor of John Heath-Stubbs; Estate of Christopher Middleton; Antoinette Moat, Estate of John Moat; Mark Pitter, Estate of Ruth Pitter; Poetry Translation Centre, representing Kajal Ahmad, Corsino Fortes, 'Gaarriye', Farzaneh Khojandi and Partaw Naderi; Estate of Nicky Rice; Estate of Vernon Scannell; Robert Sheppard, literary executor of Lee Harwood; Penelope Shuttle, Estate of Peter Redgrove; Luke Thompson and the University of Exeter, Estate of Jack Clemo; Elizabeth Wassell, Estate of John Montague; Stephen Stuart-Smith and David Whiting, literary executors of C. Day Lewis; Hamish Whyte, literary executor of Edwin Morgan; Anthony Wingfield, Viscount Powerscourt, Estate of Sheila Wingfield; Bernard Wynick, literary executor of Isaac Rosenberg.

# List of Subscribers

Norman Ackroyd

Ewa Lilian Adams

Fleur Adcock

Peter Adcock

The Adelaide Club

David Adger

Lucy Adrian

Ahsan Akbar

Jonathan Allison

Bert Almon

The late Robert Anderson

Ann Anderton

Jamie Andrews

David Archer

Anthony Astbury

Ray Atkinson and Josephine
    Cooper

Annie Auerbach and Ben Lyttleton

Jane Bailey

Margaret Bailey

Richard Bailey

William Baker

Peter Baldwin

Holly J. Ball

Kim Ballard

Peter Bamfield

Dr and Mrs C. I. Bamforth

Steve Bamlett

Ariane Bankes

Alison Barker

Martin Bax

Peter Bear

B. S. Beatty

Mary Rose Beaumont

Matthew Beaumont

Colin Beer

Raymond Bell

Nick Bellenger

Anthony Benn

Marcia Bennie

Simon Bentley

Carole Berman

Tony Bevan

Michael and Simone Bird

George Bird

David Bisset

Laurence Blackwell-Thale

The Bloomsbury Hotel

Sue Bradbury

Ben Bradshaw

Mark Brayne

Patrick Brennan

Patrick and Margaret Brittain

Isabel Brittain

Mary Broadbridge

Teresa Probert and Simon Brogan

Kate Broughton

Martin Brown

Sally Brown

Sandy Brownjohn

Brendan Bruce

Stuart Bruce

Nadine Brummer

Mhairi and Vivian Burden

Geoffrey Burgess and the late Alan
  Martin

Anne Burley

Corin Burr

Jane Burrell

Nick Burrows at
  Coombe-Hill-Books

Hanne Busck-Nielsen

Antonia Byatt

Jim and Margie Campbell

Melissa Campbell

Martin Campbell-White

Simon Caple

Trish Cardy

Philip and Christine Carne

Richard Carrington, The Poetry
  Archive

Diana and Peter Carter

Caroline Carver

David Case

John Colin Caverhill

Judith Chernaik

Kaberi Chowdhury

Neal Chuang

Hattie Clarke

Clearwater Books

Tom Cleary

Austin and Hilary Clegg

Iain and Sue Cochrane

Trevor Coldrey

John and Martin Coleman

Noel and Joan Connor

Stephen Coppel and Diana Dethloff

Caroline Cornish

Cathy Courtney and Eileen Hogan

Paul Crosbie

Graham Crossley

Gillian Crossley-Holland and
  Stephen Pattenden

Kevin Crossley-Holland

Alan Cudmore

Mara Curechian

Mark Currie and Francesca Kay

Sarah Curtis

Guy Cuthbertson

Peter Dale

Patricia Daly

Ronald Davidson-Houston

Kate Alban Davies

Graham Davies

Peter Wynne Davies

Vanessa Davis

Sean Day-Lewis

Joan Deitch

Francis J. Dempsey

Gordon Allen Dent

John Dickerson

Peter and Bridget Dickinson

Eamonn Dillon

Maura Dooley

Jane Dowson

Simon and Caroline Drew

Tom Durham

Jonathan Durrant

Vivienne Durrant

Lynda Edwardes-Evans

Eric Arthur Edwards

Richard Emeny

Jock and Charlotte Encombe

Leonard W. Erickson

John Erle-Drax

Brigitte, Felix and Max Ernst

Ronald Ewart

Ruth Fainlight

Peter Faulkner

Jane Ferguson

James Fergusson

Hamer Fernando

Sue Field Reid

Anne Vira and Aage Figenschou

Joanne Fitton

Graham Fletcher

Robynne Alison Fletcher

Duncan Forbes

Peter Forbes and Diana Reich

Claire Foster-Gilbert

Joy Francis

David Fuller

John Fuller

Richard Furniss

Jacqueline Gabbitas and Martin
    Parker

Thomas Gallant

Catriona Games

Kevin J. Gardner

Robert and Meriel Gardner

Bill Garnett

Elizabeth Garrett

Barbara and Albert Gelpi

Nick Gingell

Kenneth Glover

Mel and Rhiannon Gooding

Russell Goulbourne

David Gouldsborough

Grey Gowrie

John Graby

Nick Grant

Lavinia Greenlaw

Mary Greenslade

Chloë Greenwood

Jeremy Greenwood and Alan
    Swerdlow

John Griffith-Jones

Anja and Roland Günther

Brendan Hackett

Bernard and Patricia Haitink

Pip Hall

Iman Hallam

Holly Hamilton

Georgina Hammick

John Hampson

Richard Harms

Barbara Harvey and Stephen
    Clayson

Madeleine Heaney

Marie Heaney

Graham Henderson

Regine Henrich

Christopher and Jan Herbert

Susannah Herbert

Martin Hesketh

Mark Hinchliffe

Dr Brian Hinton

Jane Lacy Hodge

Liz Holford

Tom Holland

Alan Hollinghurst

Matthew Hollis

Jeremy Hooker

Holly Hopkins

Pat Howell

Graeme Hughes

Monzurul Huq

Bryan Robinson and Richard
    Hutchings

Stephen Huws

Monica Hying

Saul Hyman and Naomi Craft

Hamish, Julia and Aspen Ironside

Kenneth Irvine

Tristan John

Graham Johnson

Claire Jordan

Liam Keaveney

Nick and Linda Keen

Rosalind Kent

Natasha Kerr

Mark Kilfoyle

John Killick

Frances-Anne King

Catherine Kinley

Annette Kobak

Marius Kociejowski

Lotte Kramer

Shane Lalor

Nigel Lambert

Alastair Langlands

Sue Larkin

Martina Lauster and Mark
    Riddington

Christopher Le Brun PRA

Clare Lees

Jean Liddiard

Penelope Lively

Andrea Livingstone and
    Howell Huws

Dinah Livingstone

Marco Livingstone

Primrose Lockwood

Chris Lord

Andrew Louth

John and Pauline Lucas

Wendy Lynch

Matthew Macer-Wright

Catherine Mackay

Shena Mackay

Christopher MacLehose

Barbara Maddox

Maggs Bros Ltd

Barbara Mangles

John Manttan

Felicity Mara and Michael Bird

Thomas Marks

Gill Marshall-Andrews

William A. J. Martin

Penny Mason

Julian May

Neil Maybin

Alison Mayne

Rohinten Daddy Mazda

Ann and Paul McCandless

Kathryn McCandless

Joe McCann

Moy McCrory

Peter McDonald

Gary McKeone

Brian McLaughlin

Elizabeth McLaughlin

Robert McPherson

Ian Mella

Vivienne Menkès-Ivry

Henry and Alison Meyric Hughes

Margaret Miles

Paul Milliken

Mark Mills

Jeremy Mitchell

Rebecca and Paul Moisan

Charles Montgomery

Sarah Moore

Nigel Moores

Richard Morris

Sharon Morris

Peter Mortimer

Andrew J. Murch

Felicity Murdin

Peter Murray

National Poetry Library

Michael Neve

Elizabeth Newlands

Bernard and Debbie Newman

Annie Nicrow

Alastair Niven

No Alibis Bookstore

Nigel Edward Norie

Suzan Northway

Michael John Nott

Sean O'Connor

Bernard O'Donoghue

Paddy O'Hagan

Jack O'Hare

Paul O'Prey

Jennifer and Alastair O'Riordan

Michael O'Sullivan

Richard Offer

Masa Ohtake

Sue Oldershaw

Andy and Lucy Oliver

David Oliver

David Orme

Stephen Otter

Reverend Canon John Ovenden
    and Dr Christine Ovenden

Pallant House Gallery Bookshop

Nick Parfitt

Nina Parish

Angela Parobij

David Parrish

Celia Paul

James Peake

Robert Perkins

Michael Phillips

Leo Pilkington

The Poetry School

E. T. V. Poul

Neil Powell

Shahed Power

Liz and Sam Preece

Debbie Press

Roger Press

Sparrow Read

Mike and Gina Redman

Stephen Regan

Anni Reid

Michael J. Reynolds

Edward Richards

Toby Ridge

Dr R. P. A. Rivers
Gaby Robertshaw
David Robins
Mary Robins
David Robinson
Les Robinson
Pamela Robinson
Mary Robson
Christopher Rodrigues
Stephen Romer
Sten Rosenlund
Ann Rosenthal
Colin Ross
Frankie Rossi
Charlotte Rundall
David Rymill
Ines Salpico
Keith Salway
Tim and Annemarie Sayer
Myra Schneider
Richard Scott
Roger Scott
Scottish Poetry Library
Jan and Peter Selby
Liam, Kate, Abigail, Isobel and
    Nathaniel Semler
Manou Shama-Levy
Patrick Shannon
Dr Anne Sheppard
Malveen and Howard Shergold
William Sieghart
Alison Sinclair
David J. Sinclair
Juliet Singer
Lavinia Singer

Susan and John Singer
Tony Skelton
Susan Clare Smith
Philip Spedding
Sarah and David Stancliffe
Peter Stansky
G. G. T. Stanton
Jane Stemp
Anne Stewart
Seán Street
Clive Stuart-Smith
Richard Sullivan
Joyce and Nicholas Swarbrick
D. J. Taylor
Frank H. Taylor
Kim Taylor
Michael Taylor
Paul Taylor
Ruth Thackeray
Susan Thale
Richard Thomas
Peter Thompson
Roger Thorp
Andy Tickle
Roger Till
Joe and Jos Tilson
David Torrans
Lorna Tracy
Bradford Underwood
Brenda and Robert Updegraff
Janet Upward
Marina Vaizey
Charlotte Verity
Emma Wagstaff
Mette Walberg and Harald Steen

Doris Wallis
Lucile Wareing
Matthew Waterhouse
Linda Webster
Jeni Wetton
Terence Whaley
Kevin Whelan
Rupert Whitaker
David Whiting
Peter and Patricia Wightman

Jennifer Wild
Esther Williams
Graham and Nina Williams
Graeme and Iris Williamson
Peter and Greta Williamson
Rebecca Wilmshurst
Anthony and Tatty Wilson
Caroline Wiseman
David Worthington
Juliet Wrightson

Jim Dine, *Owl*, etching bound into *Kali* (1999)

David Jones, tailpiece from *The Ancient Mariner* (2006)